Certainty

Other New and Forthcoming Titles from
HACKETT
READINGS IN PHILOSOPHY

Time
Life and Death
Reality
God
Justice
The Good
Truth
Equality
Love

Certainty

Edited, with an Introduction, by
Jonathan Westphal
Idaho State University

Hackett Publishing Company, Inc.
Indianapolis/Cambridge
1995

Copyright © 1995 by Hackett Publishing Company, Inc.

Printed in the United States of America

07 06 05 04 03 02 01   2 3 4 5 6 7 8

For further information, please address

Hackett Publishing Company, Inc.
P.O. Box 44937
Indianapolis, Indiana 46244-0937

Text design by Dan Kirklin

Library of Congress Cataloging-in-Publication Data

Certainty / edited, with introductions, by Jonathan Westphal.
      p.   cm.   (Hackett readings in philosophy)
   Includes bibliographical references.
   ISBN 0-87220-319-0 (cloth: alk. paper).
   ISBN 0-87220-318-2 (pbk.: alk. paper)
   1. Certainty.   I. Westphal, Jonathan, 1951–   .   II. Series.
BD171.C46   1995
121'.63—dc20   94-44149
                                                      CIP

The paper used in this publication meets the minimum requirements of
American National Standard for Information Sciences—Permanence of
Paper for Printed Library Materials, ANSI Z39.48-1984.

Contents

Acknowledgments

I wish to thank Yvette Hebard, Ralph Baergen, Carol Hansen, Bill King, Carl Levenson, and Russell Wahl for their valuable assistance and suggestions, and also my wife, Stephanie.

Acknowledgments

For Sophie Westphal

Introduction

There is a field within philosophy, known as the theory of knowledge, which asks what knowledge is, how we get it, if we ever do, and what its importance and value are. The field is also known under the more forbidding title of *epistemology*. This word is derived from two Greek words, *episteme*, which means "a body of knowledge" or "the state of someone who possesses this knowledge," and *-logy*, which means "the study of."

Within the theory of knowledge, it has sometimes been claimed that for something to be knowledge it must be certain, though this claim has just as often been denied. Here is one way in which a certain difficult question can arise, which I shall call **Q**, for "question":

"What can I be certain of?"

Some philosophers, called *sceptics*, say that we can never be certain that anything we believe is true. Most philosophers have claimed that we can be certain of some things. Those who give the second answer to **Q** must then go on to explain the basis of their certainty, and this has proved a daunting task.

There are of course other ways in which **Q** can become important. Many people are moved to ask it by the uncertainty caused by various competing claims to knowledge. In matters of theology and religion, for example, a variety of contradictory claims are advanced. God exists; God does not exist. God loves us; God has abandoned us. One way of trying to sort out for oneself where the truth of such claims lies is to ask **Q**. If, for example, one feels certain that God exists, one might ask what it is that makes one certain, and what it is that justifies the certainty. In matters of science the question arises whether we can be certain of particular claims advanced as truths of scientific discovery or theory. Can we be certain, for example, of the truth of evolution, or the structure of DNA, or continental drift?

The writings collected in this volume revolve around **Q**, taken to cover not just individual items of alleged certainty, such as evolutionary theory and the structure of DNA, or the existence of God and of His love for us, but also the general types of knowledge to which these items belong. Is scientific knowledge ever certain? Are the truths of mathematics as certain as they seem to be? Can there also be such genuine certainty in matters of religion? Is there such a thing as the certainty of common sense? Can I ever be certain, for example, that I hear the family car coming up the drive?

Or can I only be certain of my own subjective state of consciousness, that I hear the quiet noise of gravel crunching, at the usual time, or seem to? Is certainty more than just subjective certainty, a strong feeling of conviction? Is there any such thing as objective certainty; and if there is, how can it be identified? Such questions lead naturally to a question prior to **Q**, how the term "certainty" should be analyzed. I shall call this prior question **C**:

What is certainty?

The answer to **C** involves setting a standard for certainty. What standard has to be violated to force the withdrawal of a claim to certainty? Several different answers have been given, including the most celebrated one, Descartes', which says that something is certain if it cannot be doubted.

1. Starting with Plato, philosophers have wanted to answer **Q**, and the prior question **C**, not only out of a legitimate scholarly or academic interest in the answers, but because finding out what certainty is and what we can be certain of can be a very important part of thinking out how to live and what kind of life one wants to lead. The selection from Plato's *Republic* is from a work which is very much about questions of value and how to live. Plato does not discuss certainty by name in this passage, nor does he discuss **Q** and **C** explicitly, but he argues that beyond uncertain and fallible opinion there must exist an infallible kind of knowledge which we need in order to live properly.

Infallible knowledge or science is about what is or is ultimately real. Ignorance or nescience has no object; it is not about anything, or is of what is not, as Plato puts it. Opinion or fallible belief falls between the two. It is of an unstable something which both is and is not. Plato's implicit answer to **C** is that absolutely certain knowledge is necessary and unchanging. These two characteristics derive from the involvement of knowledge in *what is*. The true philosophers should seek this certain knowledge in ultimate beauty or justice—the Forms of beauty and justice, as Plato calls them. He also calls them justice and beauty "as such," as opposed to particular just acts or beautiful objects. Particular just policies or acts can after all become unjust, and particular objects can lose their beauty, but justice itself cannot be unjust and beauty cannot itself be ugly.

2. St. Augustine was a Christian follower of Plato who shared his otherworldly orientation and wrote a huge book distinguishing an earthly city from a city of God which goes its way "a stranger on earth." St. Augustine's immediate purpose was to exculpate Christianity from the fall of Rome, the earthly city, which had lately adopted Christianity as its official religion. The tiny selection from *The City of God* is not about these large political and theological issues, but about the question of "whether you yourself exist." St. Augustine's remarkable answer is that one's own existence cannot be a deception, because if it were, there would be no one to be deceived, and hence no deception. This tricky answer to Q anticipated a more famous but very similar argument given by Descartes more than a thousand years later. Descartes argued in his *Meditations* of 1641 that if I doubt, then I think, as doubting is a form of thinking. And if I think, then I exist. So if I doubt that I exist, then I exist. Both St. Augustine and Descartes also offer a proof of the existence of God, represented as the source of all other certainties; but it is interesting to notice that for both of them the very first certainty was not the existence of God nor the Platonic world of *what is,* but the existence of someone trying to think his way out of doubt.

3. As "opinion" in Plato is a kind of belief, St. Thomas Aquinas' view, given in the selection from the *Summa Theologica,* is just the opposite of Plato's. For St. Thomas faith is more certain than science and reason, because faith is about eternal things which do not change. Yet St. Thomas says that there is a sense in which at the same time just the opposite answer can be given to Q. Since faith is about the divine, and the divine cannot be encompassed by the human intellect, the truths given by faith are less certain than truths supplied by the intellect. Absolutely or in itself, faith is more certain than reason, although, relative to reason, it is less certain. This tranquil view holds certainty and the doubting self in balance by giving two answers to C, or distinguishing two senses of "certainty." But it does raise the questions of how the truths of faith are to be identified and by what means we can have access to them and know them.

4. Descartes is regarded as the father of modern philosophy, because he made epistemology the foundation of all other philosophy,
requiring that questions of knowledge be answered before any other
philosophical question could be raised, and his view is anything but
tranquil. In the quest for certainty or indubitable truth, the reader of
his *Meditations* is plunged into uncertainty about the deliverances of
the senses, the possibility that he might be dreaming, and that an evil
demon might be causing him to think only what is false. "Archimedes
sought but one firm and immovable point in order to move the entire
earth from one place to another. Just so, great things are also to be
hoped for if I succeed in finding just one thing, however slight, that
is certain and unshaken." The storm of doubts stops abruptly with the
pronouncement that " 'I am, I exist' is necessarily true every time I
utter it or conceive it in my mind." This first certain truth, which came
to be known by philosophers as the *cogito* ("Cogito ergo sum" is Latin
for "I think, therefore I am"), cannot be doubted, for much the reason
that St. Augustine had given, and it also gives Descartes' answer to
C. Certain truths, like the *cogito,* are those which cannot be doubted
or are indubitable. The difficulty is to find anything that satisfies this
extremely strong condition. What else, beyond "I am," cannot be
doubted? This raises what the American philosopher R. B. Perry called
the "egocentric predicament." If the external world lies outside us, we
cannot know it; and if it is within us, it is not external and we have
not arrived at anything beyond ourselves.

5. The questions which Descartes introduced were taken up by
subsequent philosophers and quickly formed the mainstream of European philosophy. This is particularly true of the dreaming question.
Descartes' suggestion that if we do not know that we are not dreaming,
then the answer to Q is "Nothing" set the problem. How do we know
we are not dreaming? Leibniz's interesting answer is that waking is
distinguished from dreaming in several ways, including vividness, com-
plexity, and internal coherence. By these marks we can assure ourselves
that what we are experiencing is not a dream. "Yet the most powerful
criterion of the reality of phenomena, sufficient even by itself, is success
in predicting future phenomena from past and present ones. . . ." He
adds characteristically, "Indeed, even if this whole life were said to be
only a dream, and the visible world a phantasm, I should call this
dream or phantasm real enough if we were never deceived by it when
we make good use of reason." Yet Leibniz is realistic enough to allow

that the criteria he offers provide a "moral" but not a "metaphysical" certainty. It cannot be "demonstrated absolutely" but only with probability that physical objects or "bodies" exist.

Here Leibniz is using a received distinction. In *The Principles of Philosophy* 205–206,[1] Descartes characterizes *moral certainties* as those which have "sufficient certainty for application to ordinary life, even though they may be uncertain in relation to the absolute power of God. Thus those who have never been in Rome have no doubt that it is a town in Italy, even though it could be the case that everyone who has told them has been deceiving them." We have "*absolute* or *metaphysical certainty*" when it is wholly impossible that something should be otherwise than we judge it to be. "This certainty is based on a metaphysical foundation, namely that God is supremely good and in no way a deceiver." Descartes' claim is that we cannot err with this second kind of certainty, which he attributes to mathematics and also to our knowledge of the existence of the external world. He connects moral certainty with consistency and coherence of evidence, and the distinction is as much between two *kinds* of certainty as it is between two *degrees* of certainty. In Leibniz, however, the distinction is associated merely with degrees of probability, high and lower.

6. Leibniz's conclusion that we can only have moral certainty that we are not dreaming is perhaps a little disappointing, but nothing in comparison to the scope of David Hume's scepticism. Hume is sceptical both about Descartes' doubt, which he thinks, amusingly, is impossible for "a human creature to attain," and about Descartes' resolution of the doubt. There is no Archimedean point or first certain truth which "has a prerogative above others, that are self-evident and convincing; or if there were, could we advance a step beyond it but by the use of those very faculties of which we are supposed to be already diffident." "Trite" is what Hume calls the argument for doubt about the senses, such as the "crooked appearance of an oar in water." But he thinks he has a better argument against our natural conviction of the existence of objects external to the mind. (i) The table which we see gets smaller as we get farther away from it. (ii) The real table does not change size. Therefore (iii) it is not the real table which we see. Therefore (iv) the

---

1. Descartes, *The Principles of Philosophy*, Part IV, *The Philosophical Writings of Descartes*, Vol. I, translated by John Cottingham, Robert Stoothoff, and Dugald Murdoch, Cambridge, Cambridge University Press, 1985, pp. 289–290.

only thing that can be present to the mind is a perception or image. Yet we cannot even suppose that our perceptions are anything like the external objects that cause them, because then we would have to be in a position to compare them with these objects. "The mind never has anything present to it but the perceptions . . . ," and so there can be no basis for such a comparison. This is a version of the egocentric predicament.

7. The argument given above, from (i) and (ii) through the subconclusion (iii) to the conclusion (iv), was identified as Hume's main argument ("all I have found in Mr. Hume's writings upon this point") by Thomas Reid, a level-headed Scottish philosopher who brought a profound common sense to bear on philosophical problems. Reid says that there is a distinction between real magnitude, which is measured by units such as feet and inches, and apparent magnitude, which "is measured by the angle which an object subtends at the eye." The apparent magnitude of the diameter of the sun "is about thirty-one minutes of a degree," an angle, whereas the real magnitude is "so many thousand miles," a distance. Hume's argument (i)–(iv) overlooks this distinction. Reid also points out that if this distinction is observed, we ought to conclude that it is the real table we see, because "the table we see has precisely that magnitude which it is demonstrable the real table must have when placed at that distance." Reid thinks that here there is no basis for uncertainty.

8. The *Cartesian Meditations* are the German philosopher Edmund Husserl's reaction to Descartes' problem of finding a method for discovering certain truths, which Husserl calls "an absolute grounding of science." "Descartes himself proposed an ideal of science, the ideal approximated by geometry and mathematical natural science. As a fateful prejudice this ideal determines philosophies for centuries and hiddenly determines the *Meditations* themselves." Husserl will have none of it, seeking instead something that is "intrinsically first" or basic. Finding it is the "question of the beginning." There can be no ordinary evidence for it, but it does have something in common with ordinary evidence, "a grasping of something itself that is, or is thus, a grasping in the mode 'it itself,' with full certainty of its being." The existence of the world cannot satisfy a demand for metaphysical certainty in this idiosyncratic sense, and Husserl turns from it with the " 'parenthesizing' of the Objective world," making the claim instead

that "The world is for me absolutely nothing else but the world existing
for and accepted by me." He declares, with a touch of hauteur, that
"By my living, by my experiencing, thinking, valuing, and acting, I can
enter no world other than the one which gets its sense and acceptance
or status [*Sinn und Geltung*] in and from me. . . ."

9. There are two papers by G. E. Moore, apart from the one
included in this volume, which could have been chosen instead. They
are "A Defence of Common Sense," which Moore published in 1925,
and his 1939 British Academy Lecture "Proof of an External World."[2]
In each of the three articles Moore advances a number of propositions
or statements which he claims to know with certainty, which he also
calls "truisms." Among them are the propositions that "There exists
at present a living human body, which is *my* body"; that " . . . the earth
existed also for many years before my body was born"; and, most
famously, in the British Academy Lecture, "There is one hand and
here is another," said as he made a gesture with each of his hands. In
"Certainty" Moore begins with a similar list of propositions: "I am at
present, as you can all see, in a room and not in the open air; I am
standing up and not either sitting or lying down; I have clothes on,
and am not absolutely naked . . . ," and so on, a very clear answer
indeed to **Q**. He says that it would "sound rather ridiculous for me
now, under these circumstances, to say 'I *think* I've got some clothes
on' or even to say, 'I not only think I have, I know that it is very likely
indeed that I have, but I can't be quite sure.' " For Moore thought
that he didn't merely think he was clothed: he thought he *knew* that
he was. This is a commonsense starting point, quite the reverse of
Husserl's, in which the whole world of such known facts is placed
temporarily in abeyance. Moore's discussion is difficult, but rewarding.
He discusses, for example, a number of different senses of "certainty,"
or types of answer to **C**, including *feeling certain that* . . . , *being certain
that* . . . , *knowing for certain that* . . . , and *it being certain that.* . . . He
makes the immensely helpful point that even though the truisms are
contingent, in the sense that there is the possibility that they are false,
it does not follow that he does not know them with absolute certainty.
He also isolates for discussion the proposition that, if I don't know
that I'm not dreaming, then I don't know, e.g., that I am clothed.

2. Both articles can be found in Moore's *Philosophical Papers*, London, Allen
& Unwin, 1959.

Philosophers today have denied this type of principle (known as a "closure" principle),[3] and much fruitful discussion has ensued. Moore accepts it, but he thinks that, rather than showing absolutely that he doesn't know he is clothed, it shows equally well that he *does* know he isn't dreaming. The discussion of the dreaming question at the end of "Certainty" has Moore questioning the main points of Descartes' dreaming argument from the *Meditations*.

10. Descartes' view in the *Meditations*, before he produces the *cogito*, is sceptical. Moore's is the reverse. In answer to Q, Moore offers certainty about his truisms. To Moore's Cambridge colleague Wittgenstein, it seemed very peculiar indeed to go around saying things like, "There is one hand and here is another." "Now can one enumerate what one knows (like Moore)?" Wittgenstein asks. "Straight off like that, I believe not.—For otherwise the expression 'I know' gets misused. And through this misuse a queer and extremely important mental state seems to be revealed." We imagine ourselves going around in a cognitive state of certainty, *knowing* innumerable things, such as that we have a hand, a foot, and so on. We imagine this is in response to the doubts raised by Descartes, trying to deny the doubts. But "Doesn't one need grounds for doubt?" Though he does not mention Descartes by name, Wittgenstein is criticizing him as well as Moore. "If you tried to doubt everything, you would not get as far as doubting anything. The game of doubting itself presupposes certainty."

Wittgenstein thinks it is not right to doubt that you have a hand, when you are looking right at it. This would take some very special circumstance or ground, such as waking up in hospital after an accident and seeing one's arms in casts. One is entitled to a proper doubt that one has hands only because one is certain that one is in hospital. "[D]oubt presupposes certainty." On the other hand it is not right to insist, as one is staring straight at it, that one has a hand. One would need some special reason for saying this. It would have to be a response to something unusual which calls for it—an exclamation of joy, perhaps, after an explosion in an aeroplane. "There is one hand, and here is another. Hurrah!" But then what would it mean to say, and why would one say, and under what circumstances, "I *know* I have a hand"? By asking how one could doubt it, Wittgenstein is raising in a very special

3. See Jonathan Dancy, *Introduction to Contemporary Epistemology*, Oxford, Blackwell, 1985, pp. 10–11.

way the question **C**, what certainty actually is, in those circumstances in which its expression *is* appropriate.

11. Whatever certainty is, there is a view in which it is not worth pursuing, and is in any case impossible. Indeed, on this view it is not worth pursuing *because* it is impossible. So the answer to **Q** is, "Nothing." Apart from sceptics, this view is commonly found among enthusiasts of science who claim, with a certain smugness, that science, after all, cannot offer certainty. Reichenbach is not smug, but in the chapter from *The Rise of Scientific Philosophy* he says flat out that "We can do without certainty." And "The search for certainty had to burn itself out in the philosophical systems of the past before we were able to envisage a conception of knowledge which does away with all claims to eternal truth." Reichenbach was a member of the group known as the logical positivists which flourished in Vienna during the nineteen-twenties and -thirties, before many of its members were forced by the Nazis to emigrate to the United States and elsewhere. The positivists were hostile to metaphysics and dogma and the claims of religion, as one can tell from the chapter from Reichenbach's book. Even Reichenbach's brief remarks about the dreaming question show this scientific orientation. He starts with the idea that the division of our experiences into dream and reality is "a discovery of rather a late period in the evolution of man; we know that the primitive peoples of our day do not possess a clear delineation of the two worlds," and ends with the interesting formulation that "We cannot completely exclude the possibility that later experiences will prove that we are dreaming even now."

12. The next three philosophical selections are about dreaming and reality. Norman Malcolm, a pupil of Wittgenstein's, claims that there cannot be such a thing as not knowing whether I am awake or dreaming. It is wrong to think "being awake" is a phrase that names a state which I am permanently in except when I am asleep. Readers of Malcolm will want to connect his discussion with Wittgenstein's, especially with Wittgenstein's claim, in the *Philosophical Investigations*, that "the inner stands in need of outward criteria."

13. O. K. Bouwsma was another follower of Wittgenstein's. His "Descartes' Evil Genius" is an amusing tale about a young man, Tom, whom Descartes' evil demon tries to deceive. The demon makes a

world completely out of paper, which he tries to pass off as the real one. Tom quickly discovers that the world is a stage-set, and "He exclaims: *'Cogito me papyrum esse, ergo sum.'* He has triumphed over paperdom." So the demon makes a perfect, undetectably fake world, but he is furious and hurt when he finds himself unable to explain to Tom what the difference is between it and the real world. The demon has inadvertently created a real world! There is obviously something very sensible about Bouwsma's argument that the world cannot be a fake in absolutely every respect, because then it would be identical to the real world. Yet there is also something dissatisfying and almost superficial in this argument, and readers are invited to try to put their fingers on what it is.

14. Raymond Smullyan has been a magician as well as a mathematical logician and a musician. Students will appreciate the deftness with which he pulls together the various problems about reality, dreaming, and certainty. He accepts something like Bouwsma's conclusion, that if we are to say the world is a fake, there must be some definite and detectable respect in which it is. He adds to this the important claim, also made by Leibniz and Reichenbach, that reality and sureness are relative to future experiences. If our present experiences are stable or permanent relative to future experiences, then we can count them as real and not a dream, and, in this provisional setting, be sure of them. But the sureness is retrospective, and Smullyan claims not even to understand what absolute certainty and reality would amount to. He is a good enough philosopher, however, to allow that, though he is unsure of the notion of absolute reality, "I still sometimes have the haunting feeling that I am overlooking something crucial, that I may be missing something of extreme importance. How can I find out? God only knows! There is nothing more at present I can possibly do. But who knows? Maybe one day this idea, if there is an idea, might dawn on me."

15. The volume ends with these confessional remarks of Smullyan's, and with "Certeza," the Mexican poet Octavio Paz's reflective elegy on certainty, translated by Sharon Sieber. "From one word to the next / What I say vanishes. / I know that I am alive / Between two parentheses."

Plato, "Knowledge and Opinion," from the *Republic*

It was said by Alfred North Whitehead that all subsequent philosophy is merely a series of footnotes to Plato (428–348 B.C.). Though this is an exaggeration, Plato was one of the two great philosophical figures of classical Greece, along with Aristotle. He wrote a series of dialogues in which his teacher Socrates, who wrote nothing, is the main figure.

Then do you agree to this or not? When we say that someone desires something, do we mean that he desires everything of that kind or that he desires one part of it but not another?

We mean he desires everything.

Then won't we also say that the philosopher doesn't desire one part of wisdom rather than another, but desires the whole thing?

Yes, that's true.

And as for the one who's choosy about what he learns, especially if he's young and can't yet give an account of what is useful and what isn't, we won't say that he is a lover of learning or a philosopher, for we wouldn't say that someone who's choosy about his food is hungry or has an appetite for food or is a lover of food—instead, we'd say that he is a bad eater.

And we'd be right to say it.

But the one who readily and willingly tries all kinds of learning, who turns gladly to learning and is insatiable for it, is rightly called a philosopher, isn't he?

Then many strange people will be philosophers, for the lovers of sights seem to be included, since they take pleasure in learning things. And the lovers of sounds are very strange people to include as philosophers, for they would never willingly attend a serious discussion or

From Plato, *Republic*, translated by G.M.A. Grube, revised by C.D.C. Reeve, Indianapolis/Cambridge, Hackett Publishing Company, Inc., 1992.

spend their time that way, yet they run around to all the Dionysiac festivals, omitting none, whether in cities or villages, as if their ears were under contract to listen to every chorus. Are we to say that these people—and those who learn similar things or petty crafts—are philosophers?

No, but they are *like* philosophers.

And who are the true philosophers?

Those who love the sight of truth.

That's right, but what exactly do you mean by it?

It would not be easy to explain to someone else, but I think that you will agree to this.

To what?

Since the beautiful is the opposite of the ugly, they are two.

Of course.

And since they are two, each is one?

I grant that also.

And the same account is true of the just and the unjust, the good and the bad, and all the forms. Each of them is itself one, but because they manifest themselves everywhere in association with actions, bodies, and one another, each of them appears to be many.

That's right.

So, I draw this distinction: On one side are those you just now called lovers of sights, lovers of crafts, and practical people; on the other side are those we are arguing about and whom one would alone call philosophers.

How do you mean?

The lovers of sights and sounds like beautiful sounds, colors, shapes, and everything fashioned out of them, but their thought is unable to see and embrace the nature of the beautiful itself.

That's for sure.

In fact, there are very few people who would be able to reach the beautiful itself and see it by itself. Isn't that so?

Certainly.

What about someone who believes in beautiful things, but doesn't believe in the beautiful itself and isn't able to follow anyone who could lead him to the knowledge of it? Don't you think he is living in a dream rather than a wakened state? Isn't this dreaming: whether asleep or awake, to think that a likeness is not a likeness but rather the thing itself that it is like?

I certainly think that someone who does that is dreaming.

But someone who, to take the opposite case, believes in the beautiful itself, can see both it and the things that participate in it and doesn't believe that the participants are it or that it itself is the participants—is he living in a dream or is he awake?

He's very much awake.

So we'd be right to call his thought knowledge, since he knows, but we should call the other person's thought opinion, since he opines?

Right.

What if the person who has opinion but not knowledge is angry with us and disputes the truth of what we are saying? Is there some way to console him and persuade him gently, while hiding from him that he isn't in his right mind?

There must be.

Consider, then, what we'll say to him. Won't we question him like this? First, we'll tell him that nobody begrudges him any knowledge he may have and that we'd be delighted to discover that he knows something. Then we'll say: "Tell us, does the person who knows know something or nothing?" You answer for him.

He knows something.

Something that is or something that is not?

Something that is, for how could something that is not be known?

Then we have an adequate grasp of this: No matter how many ways we examine it, what is completely is completely knowable and what is in no way is in every way unknowable?

A most adequate one.

Good. Now, if anything is such as to be and also not to be, won't it be intermediate between what purely is and what in no way is?

Yes, it's intermediate.

Then, as knowledge is set over what is, while ignorance is of necessity set over what is not, mustn't we find an intermediate between knowledge and ignorance to be set over what is intermediate between what is and what is not, if there is such a thing?

Certainly.

Do we say that opinion is something?

Of course.

A different power from knowledge or the same?

A different one.

Opinion, then, is set over one thing, and knowledge over another, according to the power of each.

Right.

Now, isn't knowledge by its nature set over what is, to know it as it is? But first maybe we'd better be a bit more explicit.

How so?

Powers are a class of the things that are that enable us—or anything else for that matter—to do whatever we are capable of doing. Sight, for example, and hearing are among the powers, if you understand the kind of thing I'm referring to.

I do.

Here's what I think about them. A power has neither color nor shape nor any feature of the sort that many other things have and that I use to distinguish those things from one another. In the case of a power, I use only what it is set over and what it does, and by reference to these I call each the power it is: What is set over the same things and does the same I call the same power; what is set over something different and does something different I call a different one. Do you agree?

I do.

Then let's back up. Is knowledge a power, or what class would you put it in?

It's a power, the strongest of them all.

And what about opinion, is it a power or some other kind of thing?

It's a power as well, for it is what enables us to opine.

A moment ago you agreed that knowledge and opinion aren't the same.

How could a person with any understanding think that a fallible power is the same as an infallible one?

Right. Then we agree that opinion is clearly different from knowledge.

It is different.

Hence each of them is by nature set over something different and does something different?

Necessarily.

Knowledge is set over what is, to know it as it is?

Yes.

And opinion opines?

Yes.

Does it opine the very thing that knowledge knows, so that the knowable and the opinable are the same, or is this impossible?

It's impossible, given what we agreed, for if a different power is set over something different, and opinion and knowledge are different powers, then the knowable and the opinable cannot be the same.

Then, if what is is knowable, the opinable must be something other than what is?

It must.

Do we, then, opine what is not? Or is it impossible to opine what is not? Think about this. Doesn't someone who opines set his opinion over something? Or is it possible to opine, yet to opine nothing?

It's impossible.

But someone who opines opines some one thing?

Yes.

Surely the most accurate word for that which is not isn't 'one thing' but 'nothing'?

Certainly.

But we had to set ignorance over what is not and knowledge over what is?

That's right.

So someone opines neither what is nor what is not?

How could it be otherwise?

Then opinion is neither ignorance nor knowledge?

So it seems.

Then does it go beyond either of these? Is it clearer than knowledge or darker than ignorance?

No, neither.

Is opinion, then, darker than knowledge but clearer than ignorance?

It is.

Then it lies between them?

Yes.

So opinion is intermediate between those two?

Absolutely.

Now, we said that, if something could be shown, as it were, to be and not to be at the same time, it would be intermediate between what purely is and what in every way is not, and that neither knowledge nor ignorance would be set over it, but something intermediate between ignorance and knowledge?

Correct.

And now the thing we call opinion has emerged as being intermediate between them?

It has.

Apparently, then, it only remains for us to find what participates in both being and not being and cannot correctly be called purely one or the other, in order that, if there is such a thing, we can rightly call it the opinable, thereby setting the extremes over the extremes and the intermediate over the intermediate. Isn't that so?

It is.

Now that these points have been established, I want to address a question to our friend who doesn't believe in the beautiful itself or any form of the beautiful itself that remains always the same in all respects but who does believe in the many beautiful things—the lover of sights who wouldn't allow anyone to say that the beautiful itself is one or that the just is one or any of the rest: "My dear fellow," we'll say, "of all the many beautiful things, is there one that will not also appear ugly? Or is there one of those just things that will not also appear unjust? Or one of those pious things that will not also appear impious?"

There isn't one, for it is necessary that they appear to be beautiful in a way and also to be ugly in a way, and the same with the other things you asked about.

What about the many doubles? Do they appear any the less halves than doubles?

Not one.

So, with the many bigs and smalls and lights and heavies, is any one of them any more the thing someone says it is than its opposite?

No, each of them always participates in both opposites.

Is any one of the manys what someone says it is, then, any more than it is not what he says it is?

No, they are like the ambiguities one is entertained with at dinner parties or like the children's riddle about the eunuch who threw something at a bat—the one about what he threw at it and what it was in, for they are ambiguous, and one cannot understand them as fixedly being or fixedly not being or as both or as neither.

Then do you know how to deal with them? Or can you find a more appropriate place to put them than intermediate between being and not being? Surely, they can't *be* more than what is or *not be* more than what is not, for apparently nothing is darker than what is not or clearer than what is.

Very true.

We've now discovered, it seems, that according to the many conventions of the majority of people about beauty and the others, they are rolling around as intermediates between what is not and what purely is.

We have.

And we agreed earlier that anything of that kind would have to be called the opinable, not the knowable—the wandering intermediate grasped by the intermediate power.

We did.

As for those who study the many beautiful things but do not see the beautiful itself and are incapable of following another who leads them to it, who see many just things but not the just itself, and so with everything—these people, we shall say, opine everything but have no knowledge of anything they opine.

Necessarily.

What about the ones who in each case study the things themselves that are always the same in every respect? Won't we say that they know and don't opine?

That's necessary too.

Shall we say, then, that these people love and embrace the things that knowledge is set over, as the others do the things that opinion is set over? Remember we said that the latter saw and loved beautiful sounds and colors and the like but wouldn't allow the beautiful itself to be anything?

We remember, all right.

We won't be in error, then, if we call such people lovers of opinion rather than philosophers or lovers of wisdom and knowledge? Will they be angry with us if we call them that?

Not if they take my advice, for it isn't right to be angry with those who speak the truth.

As for those who in each case embrace the thing itself, we must call them philosophers, not lovers of opinion?

Most definitely.

St. Augustine, "Three Things True and Certain," from *The City of God*

St. Augustine of Hippo (354–450) flourished in North Africa. He was one of the most important of the Church Fathers, and much of both medieval theology and Protestant thought was drawn from him.

Of the image of the supreme Trinity, which we find in some sort in human nature even in its present state

And we indeed recognise in ourselves the image of God, that is, of the supreme Trinity, an image which, though it be not equal to God, or rather, though it be very far removed from Him—being neither co-eternal, nor, to say all in a word, consubstantial with Him—is yet nearer to Him in nature than any other of His works, and is destined to be yet restored, that it may bear a still closer resemblance. For we both are, and know that we are, and delight in our being, and our knowledge of it. Moreover, in these three things no true-seeming illusion disturbs us; for we do not come into contact with these by some bodily sense, as we perceive the things outside of us—colours, *e.g.*, by seeing, sounds by hearing, smells by smelling, tastes by tasting, hard and soft objects by touching—of all which sensible objects it is the images resembling them, but not themselves which we perceive in the mind and hold in the memory, and which excite us to desire the objects. But, without any delusive representation of images or phantasms, I am most certain that I am, and that I know and delight in this. In respect of these truths, I am not at all afraid of the arguments of the Academicians, who say, What if you are deceived? For if I am deceived, I am. For he who is not, cannot be deceived; and if I am deceived, by this same token I am. And since I am if I am deceived, how am I deceived in believing that I am? for it is certain that I am if

St. Augustine, *The City of God*, translated by Marcus Dodds, D.D.

I am deceived. Since, therefore, I, the person deceived, should be, even if I were deceived, certainly I am not deceived in this knowledge that I am. And, consequently, neither am I deceived in knowing that I know. For, as I know that I am, so I know this also, that I know. And when I love these two things, I add to them a certain third thing, namely, my love, which is of equal moment. For neither am I deceived in this, that I love, since in those things which I love I am not deceived; though even if these were false, it would still be true that I *loved* false things. For how could I justly be blamed and prohibited from loving false things, if it were false that I loved them? But, since they are true and real, who doubts that when they are loved, the love of them is itself true and real? Further, as there is no one who does not wish to be happy, so there is no one who does not wish to be. For how can he be happy, if he is nothing?

St. Thomas Aquinas, "Whether Faith Is More Certain Than Science and the Other Intellectual Virtues?" from the *Summa Theologica*

St. Thomas Aquinas (1225–1274) was the author of the Summa Theologica, *the great medieval synthesis of reason and faith. He has been since 1879 the official philosopher of the Roman Catholic Church.*

Whether Faith Is More Certain Than Science and the Other Intellectual Virtues?

We proceed thus: It would seem that faith is not more certain than science and the other intellectual virtues.

Objection 1. For doubt is opposed to certitude, and so a thing would seem to be the more certain through being less doubtful, just as a thing is the whiter, the less it has of an admixture of black. Now understanding, science and also wisdom are free of any doubt about their objects; but the believer may sometimes suffer a movement of doubt, and doubt about matters of faith. Therefore faith is no more certain than the intellectual virtues.

Obj. 2. Further, Sight is more certain than hearing. But *faith is through hearing* according to Rom. 10.17; but understanding, science, and wisdom imply some kind of intellectual sight. Therefore science and understanding are more certain than faith.

Obj. 3. Further, In matters concerning the intellect, the more perfect is the more certain. Now understanding is more perfect than faith, since faith is the way to understanding, according to another version of Isa. 7.9:[1] *If you will not believe, you shall not understand* (Vulg.,—

From St. Thomas Aquinas, *Summa Theologica*, translated by Fathers of the Dominican Province, Burns, Oates, and Washburn.

1. The Septuagint.

continue): and Augustine says (*De Trin.* xiv)[2] that faith is strengthened by science. Therefore it seems that science or understanding is more certain than faith.

On the contrary, The Apostle says (I Thess. 2.13): *When you had received of us the word of the hearing*, that is, by faith . . . *you received it not as the word of men, but, as it is indeed, the word of God.* Now nothing is more certain than the word of God. Therefore science is not more certain than faith; nor is anything else.

I answer that, As stated above (Part I-II, Q. LVII, A. 4, Reply 2; A. 5, Reply 3), two of the intellectual virtues are about contingent matter, namely prudence and art. Faith comes before these in point of certitude, by reason of its matter, since it is about eternal things, which never change. But the other three intellectual virtues, namely wisdom, science and understanding, are about necessary things, as stated above (Part I-II, Q. LVII, A. 5, Reply 3). But it must be observed that wisdom, science and understanding may be taken in two ways; first, as intellectual virtues, according to the Philosopher;[3] secondly, as gifts of the Holy Ghost. If we consider them in the first way, we must note that certitude can be looked at in two ways. First, on the part of its cause, and thus a thing which has a more certain cause, is itself more certain. In this way faith is more certain than those three virtues, because it is founded on the Divine truth, while the above three virtues are based on human reason. Secondly, certitude may be considered on the part of the subject, and thus the more a man's intellect lays hold of a thing, the more certain it is. In this way, faith is less certain, because matters of faith are above the human intellect, while the objects of the above three virtues are not. Since, however, a thing is judged absolutely with regard to its cause, but relatively, with respect to a disposition on the part of the subject, it follows that faith is more certain absolutely, while the others are more certain relatively, that is, for us. Likewise if these three be taken as gifts received in this present life, they are related to faith as to their principle which they presuppose, so that again, in this way, faith is more certain.

Reply Obj. 1. This doubt is not on the part of the cause of faith, but on our part, in so far as we do not fully grasp matters of faith with our intellect.

Reply Obj. 2. Other things being equal sight is more certain than

2. Chap. 1 (PL 42, 1037).
3. *Ethics*, vi, 3 (1139b15).

hearing. But if (the authority of) the person from whom we hear greatly surpasses that of the seer's sight, hearing is more certain than sight. Thus a man of little science is more certain about what he hears on the authority of an expert in science, than about what is apparent to him according to his own reason. And much more is a man certain about what he hears from God, Who cannot be deceived, than about what he sees with his own reason, which can be mistaken.

Reply Obj. 3. The gifts of understanding and knowledge are more perfect than the knowledge of faith in the point of their greater clearness, but not in regard to more certain adhering, because the whole certitude of the gifts of understanding and knowledge, arises from the certitude of faith, even as the certitude of the knowledge of conclusions arises from the certitude of the principles. But in so far as science, wisdom and understanding are intellectual virtues, they are based upon the natural light of reason, which falls short of the certitude of God's word, on which faith is founded.

4

René Descartes, "Meditations I and II and from Meditation VI," from the *Meditations*

René Descartes (1596–1650), the French philosopher and mathematician who devised the Cartesian coordinates of analytic geometry, is regarded as the father of modern philosophy. His best-known philosophical works are the Discourse on the Method *(1641), the* Meditations on First Philosophy *(1641), and the* Principles of Philosophy *(1644).*

Meditation One: Concerning Those Things That Can Be Called into Doubt

Several years have now passed since I first realized how numerous were the false opinions that in my youth I had taken to be true, and thus how doubtful were all those that I had subsequently built upon them. And thus I realized that once in my life I had to raze everything to the ground and begin again from the original foundations, if I wanted to establish anything firm and lasting in the sciences. But the task seemed enormous, and I was waiting until I reached a point in my life that was so timely that no more suitable time for undertaking these plans of action would come to pass. For this reason, I procrastinated for so long that I would henceforth be at fault, were I to waste the time that remains for carrying out the project by brooding over it. Accordingly, I have today suitably freed my mind of all cares, secured for myself a period of leisurely tranquillity, and am withdrawing into solitude. At last I will apply myself earnestly and unreservedly to this general demolition of my opinions.

Yet to bring this about I will not need to show that all my opinions

From René Descartes, *Meditations,* translated by Donald A. Cress, Indianapolis/Cambridge, Hackett Publishing Company, Inc., 1993.

are false, which is perhaps something I could never accomplish. But reason now persuades me that I should withhold my assent no less carefully from opinions that are not completely certain and indubitable than I would from those that are patently false. For this reason, it will suffice for the rejection of all of these opinions, if I find in each of them some reason for doubt. Nor therefore need I survey each opinion individually, a task that would be endless. Rather, because undermining the foundations will cause whatever has been built upon them to crumble of its own accord, I will attack straightaway those principles which supported everything I once believed.

Surely whatever I had admitted until now as most true I received either from the senses or through the senses. However, I have noticed that the senses are sometimes deceptive; and it is a mark of prudence never to place our complete trust in those who have deceived us even once.

But perhaps, even though the senses do sometimes deceive us when it is a question of very small and distant things, still there are many other matters concerning which one simply cannot doubt, even though they are derived from the very same senses: for example, that I am sitting here next to the fire, wearing my winter dressing gown, that I am holding this sheet of paper in my hands, and the like. But on what grounds could one deny that these hands and this entire body are mine? Unless perhaps I were to liken myself to the insane, whose brains are impaired by such an unrelenting vapor of black bile that they steadfastly insist that they are kings when they are utter paupers, or that they are arrayed in purple robes when they are naked, or that they have heads made of clay, or that they are gourds, or that they are made of glass. But such people are mad, and I would appear no less mad, were I to take their behavior as an example for myself.

This would all be well and good, were I not a man who is accustomed to sleeping at night, and to experiencing in my dreams the very same things, or now and then even less plausible ones, as these insane people do when they are awake. How often does my evening slumber persuade me of such ordinary things as these: that I am here, clothed in my dressing gown, seated next to the fireplace—when in fact I am lying undressed in bed! But right now my eyes are certainly wide awake when I gaze upon this sheet of paper. This head which I am shaking is not heavy with sleep. I extend this hand consciously and deliberately, and I feel it. Such things would not be so distinct for someone who is asleep. As if I did not recall having been deceived on other occasions even by similar thoughts in my dreams! As I consider these matters more carefully, I see so plainly that there are no definitive signs by which to distinguish being awake from being asleep. As a result, I am becoming quite dizzy, and this dizziness nearly convinces me that I am asleep.

Let us assume then, for the sake of argument, that we are dreaming and that such particulars as these are not true: that we are opening our eyes, moving our head, and extending our hands. Perhaps we do not even have such hands, or any such body at all. Nevertheless, it surely must be admitted that the things seen during slumber are, as it were, like painted images, which could only have been produced in the likeness of true things, and that therefore at least these general things—eyes, head, hands, and the whole body—are not imaginary things, but are true and exist. For indeed when painters themselves wish to represent sirens and satyrs by means of especially bizarre forms, they surely cannot assign to them utterly new natures. Rather, they simply fuse together the members of various animals. Or if perhaps they concoct something so utterly novel that nothing like it has ever been seen before (and thus is something utterly fictitious and false), yet certainly at the very least the colors from which they fashion it ought to be true. And by the same token, although even these general things—eyes, head, hands and the like—could be imaginary, still one has to admit that at least certain other things that are even more simple and universal are true. It is from these components, as if from true colors, that all those images of things that are in our thought are fashioned, be they true or false.

This class of things appears to include corporeal nature in general, together with its extension; the shape of extended things; their quantity, that is, their size and number; as well as the place where they exist; the time through which they endure, and the like.

Thus it is not improper to conclude from this that physics, astronomy, medicine, and all the other disciplines that are dependent upon the consideration of composite things are doubtful, and that, on the other hand, arithmetic, geometry, and other such disciplines, which treat of nothing but the simplest and most general things and which are indifferent as to whether these things do or do not in fact exist, contain something certain and indubitable. For whether I am awake or asleep, two plus three make five, and a square does not have more than four sides. It does not seem possible that such obvious truths should be subject to the suspicion of being false.

Be that as it may, there is fixed in my mind a certain opinion of long standing, namely that there exists a God who is able to do anything and by whom I, such as I am, have been created. How do I know that he did not bring it about that there is no earth at all, no heavens, no extended thing, no shape, no size, no place, and yet bringing it about that all these things appear to me to exist precisely as they do now? Moreover, since I judge that others sometimes make mistakes in matters that they believe they know most perfectly, may I not, in like fashion, be deceived every time I add two and three or count the sides of a square, or perform an even simpler operation, if that can be imagined? But perhaps God has not willed that I be deceived in this way, for he is said to be supremely good. Nonetheless, if it were repugnant to his goodness to have created me such that I be deceived all the time, it would also seem foreign to that same goodness to permit me to be deceived even occasionally. But we cannot make this last assertion.

Perhaps there are some who would rather deny so powerful a God than believe that everything else is uncertain. Let us not oppose them; rather, let us grant that everything said here about God is fictitious. Now they suppose that I came to be what I am either by fate, or by chance, or by a connected chain of events, or by some other way. But because being deceived and being mistaken appear to be a certain imperfection, the less powerful they take the author of my origin to be, the more probable it will be that I am so imperfect that I am always deceived. I have nothing to say in response to these arguments. But eventually I am forced to admit that there is nothing among the things I once believed to be true which it is not permissible to doubt—and not out of frivolity or lack of forethought, but for valid and considered reasons. Thus I must be no less careful to withhold assent henceforth even from these beliefs than I would from those that are patently false, if I wish to find anything certain.

But it is not enough simply to have realized these things; I must take steps to keep myself mindful of them. For long-standing opinions keep returning, and, almost against my will, they take advantage of my credulity, as if it were bound over to them by long use and the claims of intimacy. Nor will I ever get out of the habit of assenting to them and believing in them, so long as I take them to be exactly what they are, namely, in some respects doubtful, as has just now been shown, but nevertheless highly probable, so that it is much more consonant with reason to believe them than to deny them. Hence, it seems to me I would do well to deceive myself by turning my will in completely the opposite direction and pretend for a time that these opinions are wholly false and imaginary, until finally, as if with prejudices weighing down each side equally, no bad habit should turn my judgment any further from the correct perception of things. For indeed I know that meanwhile there is no danger or error in following this procedure, and that it is impossible for me to indulge in too much distrust, since I am now concentrating only on knowledge, not on action.

Accordingly, I will suppose not a supremely good God, the source of truth, but rather an evil genius, supremely powerful and clever, who has directed his entire effort at deceiving me. I will regard the heavens, the air, the earth, colors, shapes, sounds, and all external things as nothing but the bedeviling hoaxes of my dreams, with which he lays snares for my credulity. I will regard myself as not having hands, or eyes, or flesh, or blood, or any senses, but as nevertheless falsely believing that I possess all these things. I will remain resolute and steadfast in this meditation, and even if it is not within my power to know anything true, it certainly is within my power to take care resolutely to withhold my assent to what is false, lest this deceiver, however powerful, however clever he may be, have any effect on me. But this undertaking is arduous, and a certain laziness brings me back to my customary way of living. I am not unlike a prisoner who enjoyed an imaginary freedom during his sleep, but, when he later begins to suspect that he is dreaming, fears being awakened and nonchalantly conspires with these pleasant illusions. In just the same way, I fall back of my own accord into my old opinions, and dread being awakened, lest the toilsome wakefulness which follows upon a peaceful rest must be spent thenceforward not in the light but among the inextricable shadows of the difficulties now brought forward.

Meditation Two: Concerning the Nature of the Human Mind: That It Is Better Known Than the Body

Yesterday's meditation has thrown me into such doubts that I can no longer ignore them, yet I fail to see how they are to be resolved. It is as if I had suddenly fallen into a deep whirlpool; I am so tossed about that I can neither touch bottom with my foot, nor swim up to the top. Nevertheless I will work my way up and will once again attempt the same path I entered upon yesterday. I will accomplish this by putting aside everything that admits of the least doubt, as if I had discovered it to be completely false. I will stay on this course until I know something certain, or, if nothing else, until I at least know for certain that nothing is certain. Archimedes sought but one firm and immovable point in order to move the entire earth from one place to another. Just so, great things are also to be hoped for if I succeed in finding just one thing, however slight, that is certain and unshaken.

Therefore I suppose that everything I see is false. I believe that none of what my deceitful memory represents ever existed. I have no senses whatever. Body, shape, extension, movement, and place are all chimeras. What then will be true? Perhaps just the single fact that nothing is certain.

But how do I know there is not something else, over and above all those things that I have just reviewed, concerning which there is not even the slightest occasion for doubt? Is there not some God, or by whatever name I might call him, who instills these very thoughts in me? But why would I think that, since I myself could perhaps be the author of these thoughts? Am I not then at least something? But I have already denied that I have any senses and any body. Still I hesitate; for what follows from this? Am I so tied to a body and to the senses that I cannot exist without them? But I have persuaded myself that there is absolutely nothing in the world: no sky, no earth, no minds, no bodies. Is it then the case that I too do not exist? But doubtless I did exist, if I persuaded myself of something. But there is some deceiver or other who is supremely powerful and supremely sly and who is always deliberately deceiving me. Then too there is no doubt that I exist, if he is deceiving me. And let him do his best at deception, he will never bring it about that I am nothing so long as I shall think that I am something. Thus, after everything has been most carefully weighed, it must finally be established that this pronouncement "I am, I exist" is necessarily true every time I utter it or conceive it in my mind.

But I do not yet understand sufficiently what I am—I, who now necessarily exist. And so from this point on, I must be careful lest I unwittingly mistake something else for myself, and thus err in that very item of knowledge that I claim to be the most certain and evident of all. Thus, I will meditate once more on what I once believed myself to be, prior to embarking upon these thoughts. For this reason, then, I will set aside whatever can be weakened even to the slightest degree by the arguments brought forward, so that eventually all that remains is precisely nothing but what is certain and unshaken.

What then did I use to think I was? A man, of course. But what is a man? Might I not say a "rational animal"? No, because then I would have to inquire what "animal" and "rational" mean. And thus from one question I would slide into many more difficult ones. Nor do I now have enough free time that I want to waste it on subtleties of this sort. Instead, permit me to focus here on what came spontaneously and naturally into my thinking whenever I pondered what I was. Now it occurred to me first that I had a face, hands, arms, and this entire mechanism of bodily members: the very same as are discerned in a corpse, and which I referred to by the name "body." It next occurred to me that I took in food, that I walked about, and that I sensed and thought various things; these actions I used to attribute to the soul. But as to what this soul might be, I either did not think about it or else I imagined it a rarified I-know-not-what, like a wind, or a fire, or ether, which had been infused into my coarser parts. But as to the body I was not in any doubt. On the contrary, I was under the impression that I knew its nature distinctly. Were I perhaps tempted to describe this nature such as I conceived it in my mind, I would have described it thus: by "body," I understand all that is capable of being bounded by some shape, of being enclosed in a place, and of filling up a space in such a way as to exclude any other body from it; of being perceived by touch, sight, hearing, taste, or smell; of being moved in several ways, not, of course, by itself, but by whatever else impinges upon it. For it was my view that the power of self-motion, and likewise of sensing or of thinking, in no way belonged to the nature of the body. Indeed I used rather to marvel that such faculties were to be found in certain bodies.

But now what am I, when I suppose that there is some supremely powerful and, if I may be permitted to say so, malicious deceiver who deliberately tries to fool me in any way he can? Can I not affirm that I possess at least a small measure of all those things which I have already said belong to the nature of the body? I focus my attention on them, I think about them, I review them again, but nothing comes to mind. I am tired of repeating this to no purpose. But what about those things I ascribed to the soul? What about being nourished or moving about? Since I now do not have a body, these are surely nothing but fictions. What about sensing? Surely this too does not take place without a body; and I seemed to have sensed in my dreams many things that I later realized I did not sense. What about thinking? Here I make my discovery: thought exists; it alone cannot be separated from me. I am; I exist—this is certain. But for how long? For as long as I am thinking;

for perhaps it could also come to pass that if I were to cease all thinking I would then utterly cease to exist. At this time I admit nothing that is not necessarily true. I am therefore precisely nothing but a thinking thing; that is, a mind, or intellect, or understanding, or reason—words of whose meanings I was previously ignorant. Yet I am a true thing and am truly existing; but what kind of thing? I have said it already: a thinking thing.

What else am I? I will set my imagination in motion. I am not that concatenation of members we call the human body. Neither am I even some subtle air infused into these members, nor a wind, nor a fire, nor a vapor, nor a breath, nor anything I devise for myself. For I have supposed these things to be nothing. The assumption still stands; yet nevertheless I am something. But is it perhaps the case that these very things which I take to be nothing, because they are unknown to me, nevertheless are in fact no different from that "me" that I know? This I do not know, and I will not quarrel about it now. I can make a judgment only about things that are known to me. I know that I exist; I ask now who is this "I" whom I know? Most certainly, in the strict sense the knowledge of this "I" does not depend upon things of whose existence I do not yet have knowledge. Therefore it is not dependent upon any of those things that I simulate in my imagination. But this word "simulate" warns me of my error. For I would indeed be simulating were I to "imagine" that I was something, because imagining is merely the contemplating of the shape or image of a corporeal thing. But I now know with certainty that I am and also that all these images—and, generally, everything belonging to the nature of the body—could turn out to be nothing but dreams. Once I have realized this, I would seem to be speaking no less foolishly were I to say: "I will use my imagination in order to recognize more distinctly who I am," than were I to say: "Now I surely am awake, and I see something true; but since I do not yet see it clearly enough, I will deliberately fall asleep so that my dreams might represent it to me more truly and more clearly." Thus I realize that none of what I can grasp by means of the imagination pertains to this knowledge that I have of myself. Moreover, I realize that I must be most diligent about withdrawing my mind from these things so that it can perceive its nature as distinctly as possible.

But what then am I? A thing that thinks. What is that? A thing that doubts, understands, affirms, denies, wills, refuses, and that also imagines and senses.

Indeed it is no small matter if all of these things belong to me. But why should they not belong to me? Is it not the very same "I" who now doubts almost everything, who nevertheless understands something, who affirms that this one thing is true, who denies other things, who desires to know more, who wishes not to be deceived, who imagines many things even against my will, who also notices many things which appear to come from the senses? What is there in all of this that is not every bit as true as the fact that I exist—even if I am always asleep or even if my creator makes every effort to mislead me? Which of these things is distinct from my thought? Which of them can be said to be separate from myself? For it is so obvious that it is I who doubt, I who understand, and I who will, that there is nothing by which it could be explained more clearly. But indeed it is also the same "I" who imagines; for although perhaps, as I supposed before, absolutely nothing that I imagined is true, still the very power of imagining really does exist, and constitutes a part of my thought. Finally, it is this same "I" who senses or who is cognizant of bodily things as if through the senses. For example, I now see a light, I hear a noise, I feel heat. These things are false, since I am asleep. Yet I certainly do seem to see, hear, and feel warmth. This cannot be false. Properly speaking, this is what in me is called "sensing." But this, precisely so taken, is nothing other than thinking.

From these considerations I am beginning to know a little better what I am. But it still seems (and I cannot resist believing) that corporeal things—whose images are formed by thought, and which the senses themselves examine—are much more distinctly known than this mysterious "I" which does not fall within the imagination. And yet it would be strange indeed were I to grasp the very things I consider to be doubtful, unknown, and foreign to me more distinctly than what is true, what is known—than, in short, myself. But I see what is happening: my mind loves to wander and does not yet permit itself to be restricted within the confines of truth. So be it then; let us just this once allow it completely free rein, so that, a little while later, when the time has come to pull in the reins, the mind may more readily permit itself to be controlled.

Let us consider those things which are commonly believed to be the most distinctly grasped of all: namely the bodies we touch and see. Not bodies in general, mind you, for these general perceptions are apt to be somewhat more confused, but one body in particular. Let us take, for instance, this piece of wax. It has been taken quite recently from the honeycomb; it has not yet lost all the honey flavor. It retains some of the scent of the flowers from which it was collected. Its color, shape, and size are manifest. It is hard and cold; it is easy to touch. If you rap on it with your knuckle it will emit a sound. In short, everything is present in it that appears needed to enable a body to be known as distinctly as possible. But notice that, as I am speaking, I am bringing it close to the fire. The remaining traces of the honey flavor are disappearing; the scent is vanishing; the color is changing; the original shape is disappearing. Its size is increasing; it is becoming liquid and hot; you can hardly touch it. And now, when you rap on it, it no longer emits any sound. Does the same wax still remain? I must confess that it does; no one denies it; no one thinks otherwise. So what was there in the wax that was so distinctly grasped? Certainly none of the aspects that I reached by means of the senses. For whatever came under the senses of taste, smell, sight, touch or hearing has now changed; and yet the wax remains.

Perhaps the wax was what I now think it is: namely that the wax itself never really was the sweetness of the honey, nor the fragrance of the flowers, nor the whiteness, nor the shape, nor the sound, but instead was a body that a short time ago manifested itself to me in these ways, and now does so in other ways. But just what precisely is this thing that I thus imagine? Let us focus our attention on this and see what remains after we have removed everything that does not belong to the wax: only that it is something extended, flexible, and mutable. But what is it to be flexible and mutable? Is it what my imagination shows it to be: namely, that this piece of wax can change from a round to a square shape, or from the latter to a triangular shape? Not at all; for I grasp that the wax is capable of innumerable changes of this sort, even though I am incapable of running through these innumerable changes by using my imagination. Therefore this insight is not achieved by the faculty of imagination. What is it to be extended? Is this thing's extension also unknown? For it becomes greater in wax that is beginning to melt, greater in boiling wax, and greater still as the heat is increased. And I would not judge correctly what the wax is if I did not believe that it takes on an even greater variety of dimensions than I could ever grasp with the imagination. It remains then for me to concede that I do not grasp what this wax is through the imagination; rather, I perceive it through the mind alone. The point I am making refers to this particular piece of wax, for the case of wax in general is clearer still. But what is this piece of wax which is perceived only by the mind? Surely it is the same piece of wax that I see, touch, and imagine; in short it is the same piece of wax I took it to be from the very beginning. But I need to realize that the perception of the wax is neither a seeing, nor a touching, nor an imagining. Nor has it ever been, even though it previously seemed so; rather it is an inspection on the part of the mind alone. This inspection can be imperfect and confused, as it was before, or clear and distinct, as it is now, depending on how closely I pay attention to the things in which the piece of wax consists.

But meanwhile I marvel at how prone my mind is to errors. For although I am considering these things within myself silently and without words, nevertheless I seize upon words themselves and I am nearly deceived by the ways in which people commonly speak. For we say that we see the wax itself, if it is present, and not that we judge it to be present from its color or shape. Whence I might conclude straightaway that I know the wax through the vision had by the eye, and not through an inspection on the part of the mind alone. But then were I perchance to look out my window and observe men crossing the square, I would ordinarily say I see the men themselves just as I say I see the wax. But what do I see aside from hats and clothes, which could conceal automata? Yet I judge them to be men. Thus what I thought I had seen with my eyes, I actually grasped solely with the faculty of judgment, which is in my mind.

But a person who seeks to know more than the common crowd ought to be ashamed of himself for looking for doubt in common ways of speaking. Let us then go forward and inquire when it was that I perceived more perfectly and evidently what the piece of wax was. Was it when I first saw it and believed I knew it by the external sense, or at least by the so-called common sense, that is, the power of imagination? Or do I have more perfect knowledge now, when I have diligently examined both what the wax is and how it is known? Surely it is absurd to be in doubt about this matter. For what was there in my initial perception that was distinct? What was there that any animal seemed incapable of possessing? But indeed when I distinguish the wax from its external forms, as if stripping it of its clothing, and look at the wax in its nakedness, then, even though there can be still an error in my judgment, nevertheless I cannot perceive it thus without a human mind.

But what am I to say about this mind, that is, about myself? For as yet I admit nothing else to be in me over and above the mind. What, I ask, am I who seem to perceive this wax so distinctly? Do I not know myself not only much more truly and with greater certainty, but also much more distinctly and evidently? For if I judge that the wax exists from the fact that I see it, certainly from this same fact that I see the wax it follows much more evidently that I myself exist. For it could happen that what I see is not truly wax. It could happen that I have no eyes with which to see anything. But it is utterly impossible that, while I see or think I see (I do not now distinguish these two), I who think am not something. Likewise, if I judge that the wax exists from the fact that I touch it, the same outcome will again obtain, namely that I exist. If I judge that the wax exists from the fact that I imagine it, or for any other reason, plainly the same thing follows. But what I note regarding the wax applies to everything else that is external to me. Furthermore, if my perception of the wax seemed more distinct after it became known to me not only on account of sight or touch, but on account of many reasons, one has to admit how much more distinctly I am now known to myself. For there is not a single consideration that can aid in my perception of the wax or of any other body that fails to make even more manifest the nature of my mind. But there are still so many other things in the mind itself on the basis of which my knowledge of it can be rendered more distinct that it hardly seems worth enumerating those things which emanate to it from the body.

But lo and behold, I have returned on my own to where I wanted to be. For since I now know that even bodies are not, properly speaking, perceived by the senses or by the faculty of imagination, but by the intellect alone, and that they are not perceived through their being touched or seen, but only through their being understood, I manifestly know that nothing can be perceived more easily and more evidently than my own mind. But since the tendency to hang on to long-held beliefs cannot be put aside so quickly, I want to stop here, so that by the length of my meditation this new knowledge may be more deeply impressed upon my memory.

From Meditation Six: Concerning the Existence of Material Things, and the Real Distinction of the Mind from the Body

Next, I observe that my mind is not immediately affected by all the parts of the body, but merely by the brain, or perhaps even by just one small part of the brain—namely, by that part in which the "common sense" is said to be found. As often as it is disposed in the same manner, it presents the same thing to the mind, although the other parts of the body can meanwhile orient themselves now this way, now that way, as countless experiments show—none of which need be reviewed here.

I also notice that the nature of the body is such that none of its parts can be moved by another part a short distance away, unless it is also moved in the same direction by any of the parts that stand between them, even though this more distant part does nothing. For example, in the cord ABCD, if the final part D is pulled, the first part A would be moved in exactly the same direction as it could be moved if one of the intermediate parts, B or C, were pulled and the last part D remained motionless. Just so, when I sense pain in the foot, physics teaches me that this feeling took place because of nerves scattered throughout the foot. These nerves, like cords, are extended from that point all the way to the brain; when they are pulled in the foot, they also pull on the inner parts of the brain to which they are stretched, and produce a certain motion in these parts of the brain. This motion has been constituted by nature so as to affect the mind with a feeling of pain, as if it existed in the foot. But because these nerves need to pass through the tibia, thigh, loins, back, and neck, with the result that they extend from the foot to the brain, it can happen that the part that is in the foot is not stretched; rather, one of the intermediate parts is thus stretched, and obviously the same movement will occur in the brain that happens when the foot was badly affected. The necessary result is that the mind feels the same pain. And we must believe the same regarding any other sense. ·

Finally, I observe that, since each of the motions occurring in that part of the brain that immediately affects the mind occasions only one sensation in it, there is no better way to think about this than that it occasions the sensation that, of all that could be occasioned by it, is most especially and most often conducive to the maintenance of a healthy man. Moreover, experience shows that such are all the senses bestowed on us by nature; therefore, clearly nothing is to be found in them that does not bear witness to God's power and goodness. Thus, for example, when the nerves in the foot are violently and unusually agitated, their motion, which extends through the marrow of the spine to the inner reaches of the brain, gives the mind at that point a sign to feel something—namely, the pain as if existing in the foot. This pain provokes it to do its utmost to move away from the cause, since it is harmful to the foot. But the nature of man could have been so constituted by God that this same motion in the brain might have displayed something else to the mind: either the motion itself as it is in the brain, or as it is in the foot, or in some place in between—or somewhere else entirely different. But nothing else serves so well the maintenance of the body. Similarly, when we need a drink, a certain dryness arises in the throat that moves its nerves, and, by means of them, the inner recesses of the brain. This motion affects the mind with a feeling of thirst, because in this situation nothing is more useful for us to know than that we need a drink to sustain our health; the same holds for the other matters.

From these considerations it is totally clear that, notwithstanding the immense goodness of God, the nature of man—insofar as it is composed of mind and body, cannot help but sometimes be deceived. For if some cause, not in the foot but in some other part through which the nerves are stretched from the foot to the brain—or perhaps even in the brain itself—were to produce the same motion that would normally be produced by a badly affected foot, then the pain will be felt as if it were in the foot, and the senses will naturally be deceived, because it is reasonable that the motion should always show the pain to the mind as something belonging to the foot rather than to some other part, since an identical motion in the brain can bring about only the identical effect and this motion more frequently is wont to arise from a cause that harms the foot than from something existing elsewhere. And if the dryness of the throat does not, as is the custom, arise from the fact that drink aids in the health of the body, but from a contrary cause—as happens in the case of the person with dropsy— then it is far better that it should deceive, than if, on the contrary, it were always deceptive when the body is well constituted. The same goes for the other cases.

This consideration is most helpful, not only for noticing all the errors to which my nature is liable, but also for easily being able to correct or avoid them. To be sure, I know that every sense more frequently indicates what is true than what is false regarding those things that concern the advantage of the body, and I can almost always use more than one sense in order to examine the same thing. Furthermore, I can use memory, which connects present things with preceding ones, plus the intellect, which now has examined all the causes of error. I should no longer fear lest those things that are daily shown me by the senses, are false; rather, the hyperbolic doubts of the last few days ought to be rejected as worthy of derision—especially the principal doubt regarding sleep, which I did not distinguish from being awake. For I now notice that a very great difference exists between these two;

dreams are never joined with all the other actions of life by the memory, as is the case with those actions that occur when one is awake. For surely, if someone, while I am awake, suddenly appears to me, and then immediately disappears, as happens in dreams, so that I see neither where he came from or where he went, it is not without reason that I would judge him to be a ghost or a phantom conjured up in my brain, rather than a true man. But when these things happen, regarding which I notice distinctly where they come from, where they are now, and when they come to me, and I connect the perception of them without any interruption with the rest of my life, obviously I am certain that these perceptions have occurred not in sleep but in a waking state. Nor ought I to have even a little doubt regarding the truth of these things, if, having mustered all the senses, memory, and intellect in order to examine them, nothing is announced to me by one of these sources that conflicts with the others. For from the fact that God is no deceiver, it follows that I am in no way deceived in these matters. But because the need to get things done does not always give us the leisure time for such a careful inquiry, one must believe that the life of man is vulnerable to errors regarding particular things, and we must acknowledge the infirmity of our nature.

5

G. W. Leibniz,
"On the Method of Distinguishing Real
from Imaginary Phenomena,"
from *Philosophical Papers and Letters*

According to Bertrand Russell, Leibniz (1646–1716) "was one of the supreme intellects of all time." Leibniz discovered calculus at the same time as Newton, in a notationally superior form which is still in use today, and he is responsible for the modern concept of a function. *Among his many other contributions to philosophy, science, and theology is binary arithmetic, the simplest possible method of representing numerals. In his metaphysics, the world consists of countless nonspatial, nonphysical spiritual atoms, which he calls "monads." His concept of physical matter is that it is a function of these atoms, or a "well-founded phenomenon," as he calls it.*

A *being* is that whose concept involves something positive or that which can be conceived by us provided what we conceive is possible and involves no contradiction. We know this, first, if the concept is explained perfectly and involves nothing confused, but then in a shorter way, if the thing actually exists, since what exists must certainly be a being or be possible.

Just as being is revealed through a distinct concept, however, so existence is revealed through a distinct perception. To understand this better, we must see by what means existence may be proved. In the first place, I judge without proof, from a simple perception or experience, that those things exist of which I am conscious within me. These are, first, *myself* who am thinking of a variety of things and then, the varied *phenomena* or appearances which exist in my mind. Since both of these namely are perceived immediately by the mind without the intervention of anything else, they can be accepted without question,

From G. W. Leibniz, *Philosophical Papers and Letters*, translated by Leroy E. Loemker, Dordrecht, Kluwer Academic Publishers, 1969.

and it is exactly as certain that there exists in my mind the appearance of a golden mountain or of a centaur when I dream of these, as it is that I who am dreaming exist, for both are included in the one fact that it is certain that a centaur appears to me.

Let us now see by what criteria we may know which phenomena are real. We may judge this both from the phenomenon itself and from the phenomena which are antecedent and consequent to it as well. We conclude it from the phenomenon itself if it is vivid, complex, and internally coherent [congruum]. It will be vivid if its qualities, such as light, color, and warmth, appear intense enough. It will be complex if these qualities are varied and support us in undertaking many experiments and new observations; for example, if we experience in a phenomenon not merely colors but also sounds, odors, and qualities of taste and touch, and this both in the phenomenon as a whole and in its various parts which we can further treat according to causes. Such a long chain of observations is usually begun by design and selectively and usually occurs neither in dreams nor in those imaginings which memory or fantasy present, in which the image is mostly vague and disappears while we are examining it. A phenomenon will be coherent when it consists of many phenomena, for which a reason can be given either within themselves or by some sufficiently simple hypothesis common to them; next, it is coherent if it conforms to the customary nature of other phenomena which have repeatedly occurred to us, so that its parts have the same position, order, and outcome in relation to the phenomenon which similar phenomena have had. Otherwise phenomena will be suspect, for if we were to see men moving through the air astride the hippogryphs of Ariostus, it would, I believe, make us uncertain whether we were dreaming or awake.

But this criterion can be referred back to another general class of tests drawn from preceding phenomena. The present phenomenon must be coherent with these if, namely, it preserves the same consistency or if a reason can be supplied for it from preceding phenomena or if all together are coherent with the same hypothesis, as if with a common cause. But certainly a most valid criterion is a consensus with the whole sequence of life, especially if many others affirm the same thing to be coherent with their phenomena also, for it is not only probable but certain, as I will show directly, that other substances exist which are similar to us. Yet the most powerful criterion of the reality of phenomena, sufficient even by itself, is success in predicting future phenomena from past and present ones, whether that prediction is based upon a reason, upon a hypothesis that was previously successful, or upon the customary consistency of things as observed previously. Indeed, even if this whole life were said to be only a dream, and the visible world only a phantasm, I should call this dream or this phantasm real enough if we were never deceived by it when we make good use of reason. But just as we know from these marks which phenomena should be seen as real, so we also conclude, on the contrary, that any phenomena which conflict with those that we judge to be real, and likewise those whose fallacy we can understand from their causes, are merely apparent.

We must admit it to be true that the criteria for real phenomena thus far offered, even when taken together, are not demonstrative, even though they have the greatest probability; or to speak popularly, that they provide a moral certainty but do not establish a metaphysical certainty, so that to affirm the contrary would involve a contradiction. Thus by no argument can it be demonstrated absolutely that bodies exist, nor is there anything to prevent certain well-ordered dreams from being the objects of our mind, which we judge to be true and which, because of their accord with each other, are equivalent to truth so far as practice is concerned. Nor is the argument which is popularly offered, that this makes God a deceiver, of great importance. At least no one will fail to see how far it is from a demonstration having metaphysical certainty, for we are deceived not by God but by our judgment, asserting something without accurate proof. And though a great probability may be involved, nevertheless God, in offering us this probability, is not therefore a deceiver. For what if our nature happened to be incapable of real phenomena? Then indeed God ought not so much to be blamed as to be thanked, for since these phenomena could not be real, God would, by causing them at least to be in agreement, be providing us with something equally as valuable in all the practice of life as would be real phenomena. What if this whole short life, indeed, were only some long dream and we should awake at death, as the Platonists seem to think? Since we are destined for eternity, and this whole life, even if it were to contain many thousands of years, would be like a point with respect to eternity, how trifling a thing is this small dream, to be interposed upon such fulness of truth, to which its relation is less than that of a dream to a lifetime. Yet no reasonable person calls God a deceiver if some short dream which is completely distinct and coherent is experienced in the mind.

So far I have spoken of appearances; now we must examine those things which do not appear but which nevertheless can be inferred from appearances. It is indeed certain that every phenomenon has some cause. But if anyone says that the cause of phenomena is in the nature of our mind which contains the phenomena, he will affirm nothing false, but nevertheless he will not be telling the whole truth. For in the first place, there must necessarily be a reason why we ourselves exist rather than not. And even if we are assumed to have existed from eternity, we should still have to find a reason for eternal existence, and this reason must be sought either within the essence of our mind or outside of it. And certainly there is nothing to prevent innumerable other minds from existing as well as ours, although not all possible minds exist. This I demonstrate from the fact that all existing things are interrelated (*inter se habent commercium*). However, minds of another nature than ours can be conceived which also are interrelated with ours here. That all existing things have this intercourse with each other can be proved, moreover, both from the fact that otherwise no one could say whether anything is taking place in existence now or not, so that there would be no truth or falsehood for such a proposition, which is absurd; but also because there are no extrinsic denominations, and no one becomes a widower in India by the death of his wife in Europe unless a real change occurs in him. For every predicate is in fact contained in the nature of a subject. Now, if some possible minds exist, the question is: Why not all? Furthermore, since all existents must be interrelated, there must be a cause of their interrelations; indeed, everything must necessarily express the same nature but in a different way. But the cause which leads all minds to have intercourse with each other or to express the same nature, and therefore to exist, is that cause which perfectly expresses the universe, namely God. This cause does not have a cause and is unique. Hence it is at once clear that there exist many minds besides ours, and, since it is easy to think that men who converse with us can have exactly the same reason to doubt our existence as we have to doubt theirs; and since no reason operates more strongly for us than for them, they will also exist and have minds. Thus both sacred and profane history, and indeed whatever pertains to the status of minds or rational substances, may be considered confirmed.

Concerning bodies I can demonstrate that not merely light, heat, color, and similar qualities are apparent but also motion, figure, and extension. And that if anything is real, it is solely the force of acting and suffering, and hence that the substance of a body consists in this (as if in matter and form). Those bodies, however, which have no substantial form, are merely phenomena or at least only aggregates of the true ones.

Substances have metaphysical matter or passive power insofar as they express something confusedly; active, insofar as they express it distinctly.

6

David Hume,
"Of the Academical
or Sceptical Philosophy,"
from *An Enquiry Concerning*
Human Understanding

David Hume (1711–1776) was a Scot and a sceptic. The most astute philosopher of the eighteenth century, he is renowned for his negative analysis of causation and induction.

Of the Academical or Sceptical Philosophy

There is not a greater number of philosophical reasonings, displayed upon any subject, than those, which prove the existence of a Deity, and refute the fallacies of *Atheists;* and yet the most religious philosophers still dispute whether any man can be so blinded as to be a speculative atheist. How shall we reconcile these contradictions? The knights-errant, who wandered about to clear the world of dragons and giants, never entertained the least doubt with regard to the existence of these monsters.

The *Sceptic* is another enemy of religion, who naturally provokes the indignation of all divines and graver philosophers; though it is certain, that no man ever met with any such absurd creature, or conversed with a man, who had no opinion or principle concerning any subject, either of action or speculation. This begets a very natural question; What is meant by a sceptic? And how far it is possible to push these philosophical principles of doubt and uncertainty?

There is a species of scepticism, *antecedent* to all study and philoso-

From David Hume, *An Enquiry Concerning Human Understanding,* edited by Eric Steinberg, Indianapolis/Cambridge, Hackett Publishing Company, 1993.

phy, which is much inculcated by Des Cartes[1] and others, as a sovereign preservative against error and precipitate judgement. It recommends an universal doubt, not only of all our former opinions and principles, but also of our very faculties; of whose veracity, say they, we must assure ourselves, by a chain of reasoning, deduced from some original principle, which cannot possibly be fallacious or deceitful. But neither is there any such original principle, which has a prerogative above others, that are self-evident and convincing: or if there were, could we advance a step beyond it, but by the use of those very faculties, of which we are supposed to be already diffident. The Cartesian doubt, therefore, were it ever possible to be attained by any human creature (as it plainly is not) would be entirely incurable; and no reasoning could ever bring us to a state of assurance and conviction upon any subject.

It must, however, be confessed, that this species of scepticism, when more moderate, may be understood in a very reasonable sense, and is a necessary preparative to the study of philosophy, by preserving a proper impartiality in our judgments, and weaning our mind from all those prejudices, which we may have imbibed from education or rash opinion. To begin with clear and self-evident principles, to advance by timorous and sure steps, to review frequently our conclusions, and examine accurately all their consequences; though by these means we shall make both a slow and a short progress in our systems; are the only methods, by which we can ever hope to reach truth, and attain a proper stability and certainty in our determinations.

There is another species of scepticism, *consequent* to science and enquiry, when men are supposed to have discovered, either the absolute fallaciousness of their mental faculties, or their unfitness to reach any fixed determination in all those curious subjects of speculation, about which they are commonly employed. Even our very senses are brought

---

1. [In the *Discourse on Method* (1637) and the *Meditations* (1641), Descartes advocated a form of provisional doubt or skepticism in which "I could not do better than to try once and for all to get all the beliefs I had accepted from birth out of my mind, so that once I have reconciled them with reason I might again set up either other, better ones or even the same ones. . . . Not that I was thereby aping the sceptics who doubt merely for the sake of doubting and put on the affectation of perpetual indecision; for, on the contrary, my entire plan tended simply to give me assurance and to reject shifting ground and sand so as to find rock or clay." (*Discourse on Method* II and III).]

into dispute, by a certain species of philosophers; and the maxims of common life are subjected to the same doubt as the most profound principles or conclusions of metaphysics and theology. As these para-doxical tenets (if they may be called tenets) are to be met with in some philosophers, and the refutation of them in several, they naturally excite our curiosity, and make us enquire into the arguments, on which they may be founded.

I need not insist upon the more trite topics, employed by the sceptics in all ages, against the evidence of *sense;* such as those which are derived from the imperfection and fallaciousness of our organs, on numberless occasions; the crooked appearance of an oar in water; the various aspects of objects, according to their different distances; the double images which arise from the pressing one eye; with many other appear-ances of a like nature. These sceptical topics, indeed, are only sufficient to prove, that the senses alone are not implicitly to be depended on; but that we must correct their evidence by reason, and by considera-tions, derived from the nature of the medium, the distance of the object, and the disposition of the organ, in order to render them, within their sphere, the proper *criteria* of truth and falsehood. There are other more profound arguments against the senses, which admit not of so easy a solution.

It seems evident, that men are carried, by a natural instinct or prepossession, to repose faith in their senses; and that, without any reasoning, or even almost before the use of reason, we always suppose an external universe, which depends not on our perception, but would exist, though we and every sensible creature were absent or annihilated. Even the animal creation are governed by a like opinion, and preserve this belief of external objects, in all their thoughts, designs, and actions.

It seems also evident, that, when men follow this blind and powerful instinct of nature, they always suppose the very images, presented by the senses, to be the external objects, and never entertain any suspicion, that the one are nothing but representations of the other. This very table, which we see white, and which we feel hard, is believed to exist, independent of our perception, and to be something external to our mind, which perceives it. Our presence bestows not being on it: our absence does not annihilate it. It preserves its existence uniform and entire, independent of the situation of intelligent beings, who perceive or contemplate it.

But this universal and primary opinion of all men is soon destroyed by the slightest philosophy, which teaches us, that nothing can ever be present to the mind but an image or perception, and that the senses are only the inlets, through which these images are conveyed, without being able to produce any immediate intercourse between the mind and the object. The table, which we see, seems to diminish, as we remove farther from it: but the real table, which exists independent of us, suffers no alteration: it was, therefore, nothing but its image, which was present to the mind. These are the obvious dictates of reason; and no man, who reflects, ever doubted, that the existences, which we consider, when we say, *this house* and *that tree,* are nothing but perceptions in the mind, and fleeting copies or representations of other existences, which remain uniform and independent.

So far, then, are we necessitated by reasoning to contradict or depart from the primary instincts of nature, and to embrace a new system with regard to the evidence of our senses. But here philosophy finds herself extremely embarrassed, when she would justify this new system, and obviate the cavils and objections of the sceptics. She can no longer plead the infallible and irresistible instinct of nature: for that led us to a quite different system, which is acknowledged fallible and even erroneous. And to justify this pretended philosophical system, by a chain of clear and convincing argument, or even any appearance of argument, exceeds the power of all human capacity.

By what argument can it be proved, that the perceptions of the mind must be caused by external objects, entirely different from them, though resembling them (if that be possible) and could not arise either from the energy of the mind itself, or from the suggestion of some invisible and unknown spirit, or from some other cause still more unknown to us? It is acknowledged, that, in fact, many of these perceptions arise not from anything external, as in dreams, madness, and other diseases. And nothing can be more inexplicable than the manner, in which body should so operate upon mind as ever to convey an image of itself to a substance, supposed of so different, and even contrary a nature.

It is a question of fact, whether the perceptions of the senses be produced by external objects, resembling them: how shall this question be determined? By experience surely; as all other questions of a like nature. But here experience is, and must be entirely silent. The mind has never anything present to it but the perceptions, and cannot possibly reach any experience of their connexion with objects. The supposition of such a connexion is, therefore, without any foundation in reasoning.

To have recourse to the veracity of the supreme Being, in order to prove the veracity of our senses, is surely making a very unexpected circuit. If his veracity were at all concerned in this matter, our senses would be entirely infallible; because it is not possible that he can ever deceive. Not to mention, that, if the external world be once called in question, we shall be at a loss to find arguments, by which we may prove the existence of that Being or any of his attributes.

This is a topic, therefore, in which the profounder and more philosophical sceptics will always triumph, when they endeavour to introduce an universal doubt into all subjects of human knowledge and enquiry. Do you follow the instincts and propensities of nature, may they say, in assenting to the veracity of sense? But these lead you to believe that the very perception or sensible image is the external object. Do you disclaim this principle, in order to embrace a more rational opinion, that the perceptions are only representations of something external? You here depart from your natural propensities and more obvious sentiments; and yet are not able to satisfy your reason, which can never find any convincing argument from experience to prove, that the perceptions are connected with any external objects.

There is another sceptical topic of a like nature, derived from the most profound philosophy; which might merit our attention, were it requisite to dive so deep, in order to discover arguments and reasonings, which can so little serve to any serious purpose. It is universally allowed by modern enquirers, that all the sensible qualities of objects, such as hard, soft, hot, cold, white, black, &c. are merely secondary, and exist not in the objects themselves, but are perceptions of the mind, without any external archetype or model, which they represent. If this be allowed, with regard to secondary qualities, it must also follow, with regard to the supposed primary qualities of extension and solidity;[2] nor can the latter be any more entitled to that denomination than the former. The idea of extension is entirely acquired from the senses of sight and feeling; and if all the qualities, perceived by the senses, be in the mind, not in the object, the same conclusion must reach the idea of extension, which is wholly dependent on the sensible ideas or

2. [The distinction between primary and secondary qualities was first made by Robert Boyle (1627–1691), although the basis for the distinction goes back to ancient philosophy and is implicit in the writings of Galileo (1564–1642) and Descartes. The primary qualities are commonly understood to be those qualities of our ideas which truly characterize (or are in) the object; the secondary, those qualities of our ideas which do not truly characterize (or are not in) the object, and are, thus, merely perceptions of the mind.]

the ideas of secondary qualities. Nothing can save us from this conclusion, but the asserting, that the ideas of those primary qualities are
attained by *Abstraction*, an opinion, which, if we examine it accurately,
we shall find to be unintelligible, and even absurd. An extension, that
is neither tangible nor visible, cannot possibly be conceived: and a
tangible or visible extension, which is neither hard nor soft, black nor
white, is equally beyond the reach of human conception. Let any man
try to conceive a triangle in general, which is neither *Isosceles* nor
Scalenum, nor has any particular length or proportion of sides; and he
will soon perceive the absurdity of all the scholastic notions with regard
to abstraction and general ideas.[3]

Thus the first philosophical objection to the evidence of sense or
to the opinion of external existence consists in this, that such an opinion,
if rested on natural instinct, is contrary to reason, and if referred to
reason, is contrary to natural instinct, and at the same time carries no
rational evidence with it, to convince an impartial enquirer. The second
objection goes farther, and represents this opinion as contrary to reason:
at least, if it be a principle of reason, that all sensible qualities are in
the mind, not in the object. Bereave matter of all its intelligible qualities,
both primary and secondary, you in a manner annihilate it, and leave
only a certain unknown, inexplicable *something*, as the cause of our
perceptions; a notion so imperfect, that no sceptic will think it worth
while to contend against it.

---

3. This argument is drawn from Dr. Berkeley; [*A Treatise Concerning the
Principles of Human Knowledge*; Introduction (1710)] and indeed most of the
writings of that very ingenious author form the best lessons of scepticism,
which are to be found either among the ancient or modern philosophers,
Bayle not excepted. He professes, however, in his title-page (and undoubtedly
with great truth) to have composed his book against the sceptics as well as
against the atheists and free-thinkers. But that all his arguments, though
otherwise intended, are, in reality, merely sceptical, appears from this, *that
they admit of no answer and produce no conviction*. Their only effect is to cause
that momentary amazement and irresolution and confusion, which is the result
of scepticism.

7

Thomas Reid, "Reflections on the Common Theory of Ideas," from the *Essays on the Intellectual Powers of Man*

Thomas Reid (1710–1796) was the founder of the Scottish school of common-sense philosophy. Earlier than any other philosopher, he formulated the insight that the sceptical conclusions of Hume had their origin in the theory of ideas shared by Hume's predecessors from Descartes on. This theory claimed that we are only ever directly aware of our own "ideas" or perceptions, and that any mental act must have for its object these "ideas," not something in the external world.

There remains only one other argument that I have been able to find urged against our perceiving external objects immediately. It is proposed by Mr. Hume, who, in the Essay already quoted, after acknowledging that it is an universal and primary opinion of all men, that we perceive external objects immediately, subjoins what follows:

"But this universal and primary opinion of all men is soon destroyed by the slightest philosophy, which teaches us, that nothing can ever be present to the mind but an image or perception; and that the senses are only the inlets through which these images are received, without being ever able to produce any immediate intercourse between the mind and the object. The table, which we see, seems to diminish as we remove further from it; but the real table, which exists independent of us, suffers no alteration. It was therefore nothing but its image which was present to the mind. These are the obvious dictates of reason; and no man who reflects, ever doubted that the existences which we

Thomas Reid, *Essays on the Intellectual Powers of Man*, 1785.

consider, when we say, *this house*, and *that tree*, are nothing but perceptions in the mind, and fleeting copies and representations of other
existences, which remain uniform and independent. So far then, we
are necessitated, by reasoning, to depart from the primary instincts of
nature, and to embrace a new system, with regard to the evidence of
our senses."

We have here a remarkable conflict between two contradictory opinions, wherein all mankind are engaged. On the one side, stand all the
vulgar, who are unpractised in philosophical researches, and guided
by the uncorrupted primary instincts of nature. On the other side,
stand all the philosophers ancient and modern; every man without
exception who reflects. In this division, to my great humiliation, I find
myself classed with the vulgar.

The passage now quoted is all I have found in Mr. Hume's writings
upon this point; and indeed there is more reasoning in it than I have
found in any other author; I shall therefore examine it minutely.

First, He tells us, That "this universal and primary opinion of all
men is soon destroyed by the slightest philosophy, which teaches us, that
nothing can ever be present to the mind but an image or perception."

The phrase of being present to the mind has some obscurity: but I
conceive he means being an immediate object of thought; an immediate
object, for instance, of perception, of memory, or of imagination. If
this be the meaning, and it is the only pertinent one I can think of,
there is no more in this passage but an assertion of the proposition to
be proved, and an assertion that philosophy teaches it. If this be so, I
beg leave to dissent from philosophy till she gives me reason for what
she teaches. For though common sense and my external senses demand
my assent to their dictates upon their own authority, yet philosophy is
not entitled to this privilege. But that I may not dissent from so grave
a personage without giving a reason, I give this as the reason of my
dissent. I see the sun when he shines; I remember the battle of Cullo-
den; and neither of these objects is an image or perception.

He tells us in the *next* place, "That the senses are only the inlets
through which these images are received."

I know that Aristotle and the schoolmen taught, that images or
species flow from objects, and are let in by the senses, and strike upon
the mind; but this has been so effectually refuted by Des Cartes, by
Malebranche, and many others, that nobody now pretends to defend
it. Reasonable men consider it as one of the most unintelligible and
unmeaning parts of the ancient system. To what cause is it owing that

modern philosophers are so prone to fall back into this hypothesis, as if they really believed it? For of this proneness I could give many instances besides this of Mr. Hume; and I take the cause to be, that images in the mind, and images let in by the senses, are so nearly allied, and so strictly connected, that they must stand or fall together. The old system consistently maintained both: but the new system has rejected the doctrine of images let in by the senses, holding, nevertheless, that there are images in the mind; and, having made this unnatural divorce of two doctrines which ought not to be put asunder, that which they have retained often leads them back involuntarily to that which they have rejected.

Mr. Hume surely did not seriously believe that an image of sound is let in by the ear, an image of smell by the nose, an image of hardness and softness, of solidity and resistance, by the touch. For, besides the absurdity of the thing, which has often been shown, Mr. Hume, and all modern philosophers maintain, that the images which are the immediate objects of perception, have no existence when they are not perceived; whereas, if they were let in by the senses, they must be, before they are perceived, and have a separate existence.

He tells us further, that philosophy teaches, that the senses are unable to produce any immediate intercourse between the mind and the object. Here I still require the reasons that philosophy gives for this; for, to my apprehension, I immediately perceive external objects, and this I conceive is the immediate intercourse here meant.

Hitherto I see nothing that can be called an argument. Perhaps it was intended only for illustration. The argument, the only argument follows:

The table, which we see, seems to diminish as we remove further from it; but the real table, which exists independent of us, suffers no alteration. It was therefore nothing but its image which was presented to the mind. These are the obvious dictates of reason.

To judge of the strength of this argument, it is necessary to attend to a distinction which is familiar to those who are conversant in the mathematical sciences, I mean the distinction between real and apparent magnitude. The real magnitude of a line is measured by some known measure of length, as inches, feet, or miles. The real magnitude of a surface or solid, by known measures of surface or of capacity. This magnitude is an object of touch only, and not of sight; nor could we even have had any conception of it, without the sense of touch; and Bishop Berkeley, on that account, calls it *tangible magnitude*.

Apparent magnitude is measured by the angle which an object subtends at the eye. Supposing two right lines drawn from the eye to the extremities of the object, making an angle, of which the object is the subtense, the apparent magnitude is measured by this angle. This apparent magnitude is an object of sight, and not of touch. Bishop Berkeley calls it *visible magnitude*.

If it be asked, What is the apparent magnitude of the sun's diameter? the answer is, That it is about thirty-one minutes of a degree. But if it be asked, What is the real magnitude of the sun's diameter? The answer must be, So many thousand miles, or so many diameters of the earth. From which it is evident, that real magnitude, and apparent magnitude, are things of a different nature, though the name of magnitude is given to both. The first has three dimensions, the last only two. The first is measured by a line, the last by an angle.

From what has been said, it is evident that the real magnitude of a body must continue unchanged, while the body is unchanged. This we grant. But is it likewise evident, that the apparent magnitude must continue the same while the body is unchanged? So far otherwise, that every man who knows any thing of mathematics can easily demonstrate, that the same individual object, remaining in the same place, and unchanged, must necessarily vary in its apparent magnitude, according as the point from which it is seen is more or less distant; and that its apparent length or breadth will be nearly in a reciprocal proportion to the distance of the spectator. This is as certain as the principles of geometry.

We must likewise attend to this, that though the real magnitude of a body is not originally an object of sight, but of touch, yet we learn by experience to judge of the real magnitude in many cases by sight. We learn by experience to judge of the distance of a body from the eye within certain limits; and from its distance and apparent magnitude taken together, we learn to judge of its real magnitude.

And this kind of judgment, by being repeated every hour, and almost every minute of our lives, becomes, when we are grown up, so ready and so habitual, that it very much resembles the original perceptions of our senses, and may not improperly be called *acquired perception*.

Whether we call it judgment or acquired perception is a verbal difference. But it is evident, that, by means of it, we often discover by one sense things which are properly and naturally the objects of another. Thus I can say without impropriety, I hear a drum, I hear a great bell, or I hear a small bell; though it is certain that the figure or size of the sounding body is not originally an object of hearing. In like manner, we learn by experience how a body of such a real magnitude, and at such a distance, appears to the eye: but neither its real magnitude, nor its distance from the eye, are properly objects of sight, any more than the form of a drum, or the size of a bell, are properly objects of hearing.

If these things be considered, it will appear, that Mr. Hume's argument has no force to support his conclusion, nay, that it leads to a contrary conclusion. The argument is this. The table we see, seems to diminish as we remove further from it; that is, its apparent magnitude is diminished; but the real table suffers no alteration, to wit, in its real magnitude; therefore it is not the real table we see. I admit both the premises in this syllogism, but I deny the conclusion. The syllogism has what the logicians call two middle terms. Apparent magnitude is the middle term in the first premise; real magnitude in the second. Therefore, according to the rules of logic, the conclusion is not justly drawn from the premises; but, laying aside the rules of logic, let us examine it by the light of common sense.

Let us suppose, for a moment, that it is the real table we see. Must not this real table seem to diminish as we remove further from it? It is demonstrable that it must. How then can this apparent diminution be an argument that it is not the real table? When that which must happen to the real table, as we remove further from it, does actually happen to the table we see, it is absurd to conclude from this, that it is not the real table we see. It is evident, therefore, that this ingenious author has imposed upon himself, by confounding real magnitude with apparent magnitude, and that his argument is a mere sophism.

I observed that Mr. Hume's argument, not only has no strength to support his conclusion, but that it leads to the contrary conclusion; to wit, that it is the real table we see; for this plain reason, that the table we see has precisely that apparent magnitude which it is demonstrable the real table must have when placed at that distance.

The argument is made much stronger by considering, that the real table may be placed successively at a thousand different distances, and in every distance, in a thousand different positions; and it can be determined demonstratively, by the rules of geometry and perspective, what must be its apparent magnitude, and apparent figure, in each of those distances and positions. Let the table be placed successively in as many of these different distances, and different positions, as you will, or in them all; open your eyes, and you shall see a table precisely of that apparent magnitude, and that apparent figure, which the real table must have in that distance, and in that position. Is not this a strong argument that it is the real table you see?

In a word, the appearance of a visible object is infinitely diversified, according to its distance and position. The visible appearances are innumerable, when we confine ourselves to one object, and they are multiplied according to the variety of objects. Those appearances have been matter of speculation to ingenious men, at least since the time of Euclid. They have accounted for all this variety, on the supposition, that the objects we see are external, and not in the mind itself. The rules they have demonstrated about the various projections of the sphere, about the appearances of the planets in their progressions, stations, and retrogradations, and all the rules of perspective, are built on the supposition that the objects of sight are external. They can each of them be tried in thousands of instances. In many arts and professions, innumerable trials are daily made; nor were they ever found to fail in a single instance. Shall we say that a false supposition, invented by the rude vulgar, has been so lucky in solving an infinite number of phenomena of nature? This surely would be a greater prodigy than philosophy ever exhibited. Add to this, that upon the contrary hypothesis, to wit, that the objects of sight are internal, no account can be given of any one of those appearances, nor any physical cause assigned why a visible object should, in any one case, have one apparent figure and magnitude rather than another.

Thus I have considered every argument I have found advanced to prove the existence of ideas or images of external things in the mind; and if no better arguments can be found, I cannot help thinking, that the whole history of philosophy has never furnished an instance of an opinion so unanimously entertained by philosophers upon so slight grounds.

8

Edmund Husserl, "First Meditation: the Way to the Transcendental Ego," from *Cartesian Meditations*

Edmund Husserl (1859–1938) was the European or Continental philosopher who founded phenomenology. *In this philosophy the reality of things is temporarily set aside or "bracketed" or "parenthesized" in order to allow a description of their manifestation in consciousness. Husserl was the author of* Logical Investigations *(1900–1901),* Ideas *(1913), and* The Crisis of the European Sciences *(1938).*

The Cartesian Overthrow and the Guiding Final Idea of an Absolute Grounding of Science.

And so we make a new beginning, each for himself and in himself, with the decision of philosophers who begin radically: that at first we shall put out of action all the convictions we have been accepting up to now, including all our sciences. Let the idea guiding our meditations be at first the Cartesian idea of a science that shall be established as radically genuine, ultimately an all-embracing science.

But, now that we no longer have at our disposal any already-given science as an example of radically genuine science (after all, we are not accepting any given science), what about the indubitability of that idea itself, the idea namely of a science that shall be grounded absolutely? Is it a legitimate final idea, the possible aim of some possible practice? Obviously that too is something we must not presuppose, to say nothing of taking any norms as already established for testing such possibilities—or perchance a whole system of norms in which the style proper to genuine science is allegedly prescribed. That would mean

From Edmund Husserl, *Cartesian Meditations*, translated by Dorion Cairns, The Hague, Nijhoff, 1969. Reprinted by permission of Kluwer Academic Publishers.

presupposing a whole logic as a theory of science; whereas logic must be included among the sciences overthrown in overthrowing all science. Descartes himself presupposed an ideal of science, the ideal approximated by geometry and mathematical natural science. As a fateful prejudice this ideal determines philosophies for centuries and hiddenly determines the *Meditations* themselves. Obviously it was, for Descartes, a truism from the start that the all-embracing science must have the form of a deductive system, in which the whole structure rests, *ordine geometrico*, on an axiomatic foundation that grounds the deduction absolutely. For him a role similar to that of geometrical axioms in geometry is played in the all-embracing science by the axiom of the ego's absolute certainty of himself, along with the axiomatic principles innate in the ego—only this axiomatic foundation lies even deeper than that of geometry and is called on to participate in the ultimate grounding even of geometrical knowledge.

None of that shall determine our thinking. As beginning philosophers we do not as yet accept any normative ideal of science; and only so far as we produce one newly for ourselves can we ever have such an ideal.

But this does not imply that we renounce the general aim of grounding science absolutely. That aim shall indeed continually motivate the course of our meditations, as it motivated the course of the Cartesian meditations; and gradually, in our meditations, it shall become determined concretely. Only we must be careful about how we make an absolute grounding of science our aim. At first we must not presuppose even its possibility. How then are we to find the legitimate manner in which to make it our aim? How are we to make our aim perfectly assured, and thus assured as a practical possibility? How are we then to differentiate the possibility, into which at first we have a general insight, and thereby mark out the determinate methodical course of a genuine philosophy, a radical philosophy that begins with what is intrinsically first?

Naturally we get the general idea of science from the sciences that are factually given. If they have become for us, in our radical critical attitude, merely alleged sciences, then, according to what has already been said, their general final idea has become, in a like sense, a mere supposition. Thus we do not yet know whether that idea is at all capable of becoming actualized. Nevertheless we do have it in this form, and in a state of indeterminate fluid generality; accordingly we have also the idea of philosophy: as an idea about which we do not know whether or how it can be actualized. We take the general idea of science, therefore, as a precursory presumption, which we allow ourselves tentatively, by which we tentatively allow ourselves to be guided in our meditations. We consider how it might be thought out as a possibility and then consider whether and how it might be given determinate actualization. To be sure, we get into what are, at first, rather strange circumstantialities—but how can they be avoided, if our radicalness is not to remain an empty gesture but is to become an actual deed? Let us go on then with patience.

Uncovering the Final Sense of Science by Becoming Immersed in Science Qua Noematic Phenomenon.

Obviously one of the first things we must do now is make distinct the guiding idea that, at the beginning, floats before us as a vague generality. The genuine concept of science, naturally, is not to be fashioned by a process of abstraction based on comparing the de facto sciences, i.e. the Objectively documented theoretical structures (propositions, theories) that are in fact generally accepted as sciences. The sense of our whole meditation implies that sciences, as these facts of Objective culture, and sciences "in the true and genuine sense" need not be identical and that the former, over and above being cultural facts, involve a claim, which ought to be established as one they already satisfy. Science as an idea—as the idea, genuine science—"lies", still undisclosed, precisely in this claim.

How can this idea be uncovered and apprehended? Even though we must not take any position with respect to the *validity* of the de facto sciences (the ones "claiming" validity)—i.e. with respect to the genuineness of their theories and, correlatively, the competence of their methods of theorizing—there is nothing to keep us from "immersing ourselves" in the scientific striving and doing that pertain to them, in order to see clearly and distinctly what is really being aimed at. If we do so, if we immerse ourselves progressively in the characteristic intention of scientific endeavor, the constituent parts of the general final idea, genuine science, become explicated for us, though at first the differentiation is itself general.

Here belongs, first of all, an initial clarification of *"judicative" doing* and the *"judgment" itself,* along with the discrimination of *immediate and mediate judgments:* mediate judgments have such a sense-relatedness to other judgments that judicatively believing them "presupposes" believing these others—in the manner characteristic of a believing on account of something believed already. Also clarification of the striving for *grounded judgments*, clarification of the grounding doing, in which the "*correctness*", the "*truth*", of the judgment should be shown—or, in case of a failure, the incorrectness, the falsity, of the judgment. Where mediate judgments are concerned, this showing is itself mediate; it rests on the showing that pertains to the immediate judgments involved in the judgment-sense and, as concrete, includes their grounding too. To a grounding already executed, or to the truth shown therein, one can "return" at will. By virtue of this freedom to reactualize such a truth, with awareness of it as one and the same, it is an abiding acquisition or possession and, as such, is called a *cognition*.

If we go further in this manner (here, naturally, we are only indicating the procedure), then, in explicating more precisely the sense of a grounding or that of a cognition, we come forthwith to the idea of *evidence*. In a genuine grounding, judgments show themselves as "correct", as "agreeing"; that is to say, the grounding is an *agreement* of the judgment with the judged state of affairs [*Urteilsverhalt*] (the affair or affair-complex [*Sachverhalt*]) "itself". More precisely stated: Judging is meaning—and, as a rule, merely supposing—that such and such exists and has such and such determinations; the judgment (what is judged) is then a merely supposed affair or complex of affairs: an affair, or state-of-affairs, as what is meant. But, contrasted with that, there is sometimes a pre-eminent judicative meaning [*Meinen*], a judicative having of such and such itself. This having is called *evidence*. In it the affair, the complex (or state) of affairs, instead of being merely meant "from afar", is present as the affair "itself", the *affair-complex or state-of-affairs "itself"*; the judger accordingly possesses it itself. A merely supposing judging *becomes adjusted* to the affairs, the affair-complexes, themselves by conscious conversion into the corresponding evidence. This conversion is inherently characterized as the fulfilling of what was merely meant, a synthesis in which what was meant coincides and agrees with what is itself given; it is an evident possessing of the correctness of what previously was meant at a distance from affairs.

When we proceed thus, fundamental components of the final idea governing all scientific doing come immediately to the fore. For example, the scientist intends, not merely to judge, but to ground his judgments. Stated more precisely: He intends to let no judgment be accepted by himself or others as "scientific knowledge", unless he has grounded it perfectly and can therefore justify it completely at any time by a freely actualizable return to his repeatable act of grounding. De facto that may never go beyond being a mere claim; at all events, the claim involves an ideal goal.

Yet there is one more thing that should be brought out, to supplement what we have said. We must distinguish the judgment in the broadest sense (something meant as being) and evidence in the broadest sense from pre-predicative judgment and from pre-predicative evidence respectively. Predicative includes pre-predicative evidence. That which is meant or, perchance, evidently viewed receives predicative expression; and science always intends to judge expressly and keep the judgment or the truth fixed, as an express judgment or as an express truth. But the expression as such has its own comparatively good or bad way of fitting what is meant or itself given; and therefore it has its own evidence or non-evidence, which also goes into the predicating. Consequently evidence of the expression is also a determining part of the idea of scientific truth, as predicative complexes that are, or can be, grounded absolutely.

Evidence and the Idea of Genuine Science.

As we go on meditating in this manner and along this line, we beginning philosophers recognize that the Cartesian idea of a science (ultimately an all-embracing science) grounded on an absolute foundation, and absolutely justified, is none other than the idea that constantly furnishes guidance in all sciences and in their striving toward universality— whatever may be the situation with respect to a de facto actualization of that idea.

Evidence is, in an *extremely broad sense*, an "*experiencing*" of something that is, and is thus; it is precisely a mental seeing of something itself. Conflict with what evidence shows, with what "experience" shows, yields the negative of evidence (or negative evidence)—put in the form of a judgment: positive evidence of the affair's non-being. In other words, negative evidence has as its content evident falsity. Evidence, which in fact includes all experiencing in the usual and narrower sense, can be more or less perfect. *Perfect evidence* and its correlate, *pure and genuine truth*, are given as ideas lodged in the striving for knowledge, for fulfillment of one's meaning intention. By immersing ourselves in such a striving, we can extract those ideas from it. Truth and falsity, criticism and critical comparison with evident data, are an everyday theme, playing their incessant part even in prescientific life. For this everyday life, with its changing and relative purposes, relative evidences and truths suffice. But science looks for truths that are valid, and remain so, *once for all and for everyone;* accordingly it seeks verifications of a new kind, verifications carried through to the end. Though de facto, as science itself must ultimately see, it does not attain actualization of a system of absolute truths, but rather is obliged to modify its "truths" again and again, it nevertheless follows the idea of absolute or scientifically genuine truth; and accordingly it reconciles itself to an infinite horizon of approximations, tending toward that idea. By them, science believes, it can surpass *in infinitum* not only everyday knowing but also itself; likewise however by its aim at systematic universality of knowledge, whether that aim concern a particular closed scientific province or a presupposed all-embracing unity of whatever exists— as it does if a "philosophy" is possible and in question. According to intention, therefore, the idea of science and philosophy involves an *order of cognition, proceeding from intrinsically earlier to intrinsically later cognitions;* ultimately, then, *a beginning and a line of advance* that are not to be chosen arbitrarily but have their basis "in the nature of things themselves".

Thus, by immersing ourselves meditatively in the general intentions of scientific endeavor, we discover fundamental parts of the final idea, genuine science, which, though vague at first, governs that striving. Meanwhile we have made no advance judgment in favor of the possibility of those components or in favor of a supposedly unquestionable scientific ideal.

We must not say at this point: "Why bother with such investigations and ascertainments? They obviously belong to the general theory of science, to logic, which must of course be applied both now and later." On the contrary, we must guard ourselves against just this matter-of-course opinion. Let us emphasize what we said against Descartes: Like every other already-given science, logic is deprived of acceptance by the universal overthrow. Everything that makes a philosophical beginning possible we must first acquire by ourselves. Whether, later on, a genuine science similar to traditional logic will accrue to us is an eventuality about which we can at present know nothing.

By this preliminary work, here roughly indicated rather than done explicitly, we have gained a measure of clarity sufficient to let us fix, for our whole further procedure, a *first methodological principle*. It is plain that I, as someone beginning philosophically, since I am striving toward the presumptive end, genuine science, must neither make nor go on accepting any judgment as scientific *that I have not derived from evidence*, from "experiences" in which the affairs and affair-complexes in question are present to me as "*they themselves*". Indeed, even then I must at all times reflect on the pertinent evidence; I must examine its "range" and make evident to myself *how far* that evidence, how far its "perfection," *the actual giving of the affairs themselves*, extends. Where this is still wanting, I must not claim any final validity, but must account my judgment as, at best, a possible intermediate stage on the way to final validity.

Because the sciences aim at predications that express completely and with evident fitness what is beheld pre-predicatively, it is obvious that I must be careful also about this aspect of scientific evidence. Owing to the instability and ambiguity of common language and its much too great complacency about completeness of expression, we require, even where we use its means of expression, a new legitimation of significations by orienting them according to accrued insights, and a fixing of words as expressing the significations thus legitimated. That too we account as part of our normative principle of evidence, which we shall apply consistently from now on.

But how would this principle, or all our meditation up to now, help us, if it gave us no hold for making an actual beginning, that is, for starting to actualize the idea of genuine science? Since the form belonging to a systematic order of cognitions—genuine cognitions—is part of this idea, there emerges, as the *question of the beginning*, the inquiry for those cognitions that are first in themselves and can support the whole storied edifice of universal knowledge. Consequently, if our presumptive aim is to be capable of becoming a practically possible one, we meditators, while completely destitute of all scientific knowledge, must have access to evidences that already bear the stamp of fitness for such a function, in that they are recognizable as preceding all other imaginable evidences. Moreover, in respect of this evidence of preceding, they must have a certain perfection, they must carry with them an absolute certainty, if advancing from them and constructing on their basis a science governed by the idea of a definitive system of knowledge—considering the infinity presumed to be part of this idea— is to be capable of having any sense.

Differentiations of Evidence. The Philosophical Demand for an Evidence That Is Apodictic and First in Itself.

But here, at this decisive point in the process of beginning, we must penetrate deeper with our meditations. The phrase *absolute certainty* and the equivalent phrase *absolute indubitability* need clarifying. They call our attention to the fact that, on more precise explication, the ideally demanded *perfection of evidence becomes differentiated.* At the present introductory stage of philosophical meditation we have the boundless infinity of prescientific experiences, evidences: more or less perfect. With reference to them *imperfection,* as a rule, signifies *incompleteness,* a one-sidedness and at the same time a relative obscurity and indistinctness that qualify the givenness of the affairs themselves or the affair-complexes themselves: i.e., an infectedness of the "experience" with *unfulfilled components,* with *expectant* and *attendant meanings.* Perfecting then takes place as a synthetic course of further harmonious experiences in which these attendant meanings become fulfilled in actual experience. The corresponding idea of perfection would be that of "*adequate evidence*"—and the question whether adequate evidence does not necessarily lie at infinity may be left open.

Though this idea continuously guides the scientist's intent, *a different perfection* of evidence has for him (as we see by the aforesaid process of "immersing ourselves" in his intent) a higher dignity. This perfection is "*apodicticity*"; and it can occur even in evidences that are inadequate. It is *absolute indubitability* in a quite definite and peculiar sense, the absolute indubitability that the scientist demands of all "*principles*"; and its superior value is evinced in his endeavor, where groundings already evident in and by themselves are concerned, to ground them further and at a higher level by going back to principles, and thereby to obtain for them the highest dignity, that of apodicticity. The fundamental nature of apodicticity can be characterized in the following manner:

Any evidence is a grasping of something itself that is, or is thus, a grasping in the mode "it itself", with full certainty of its being, a certainty that accordingly excludes every doubt. But it does not follow that full certainty excludes the conceivability that what is evident could subsequently become doubtful, or the conceivability that being could prove to be illusion—indeed, sensuous experience furnishes us with cases where that happens. Moreover, this open possibility of becoming doubtful, or of non-being, *in spite of evidence,* can always be recognized in advance by critical reflection on what the evidence in question does.

An *apodictic* evidence, however, is not merely certainty of the affairs or affair-complexes (states-of-affairs) evident in it; rather it discloses itself, to a critical reflection, as having the signal peculiarity of being *at the same time the absolute unimaginableness* (inconceivability) of their *non-being,* and thus excluding in advance every doubt as "objectless", empty. Furthermore the evidence of that critical reflection likewise has the dignity of being apodictic, as does therefore the evidence of the unimaginableness of what is presented with apodictically evident certainty. And the same is true of every critical reflection at a higher level.

We remember now the Cartesian principle for building genuine science: the principle of absolute indubitability, by which every imaginable doubt (even though it were in fact groundless) was to be excluded. If, by our meditations, we have acquired that principle in a clarified form, there arises the question whether and how it might help us make an actual beginning. In accordance with what has already been said, we now formulate, as an initial definite question of beginning philosophy, the question whether it is possible for us to bring out evidences that, on the one hand, carry with them—as we now must say: apodictically—the insight that, as "first in themselves", they precede all other imaginable evidences and, on the other hand, can be seen to be themselves apodictic. If they should turn out to be inadequate, they would have to possess at least a recognizable apodictic content, they would have to give us some being that is firmly secured "once for all", or absolutely, by virtue of their apodicticity. *How,* and even *whether,* it would be possible to go on from there and build an apodictically secured philosophy must, of course, remain for later consideration.

The Evidence for the Factual Existence of the World Not Apodictic; Its Inclusion in the Cartesian Overthrow.

The question of evidences that are first in themselves can apparently be answered without any trouble. Does not the *existence of the world* present itself forthwith as such an evidence? The life of everyday action relates to the world. All the sciences relate to it: the sciences of matters of fact relate to it immediately; the apriori sciences, mediately, as instruments of scientific method. More than anything else the being of the world is obvious. It is so very obvious that no one would think of asserting it expressly in a proposition. After all, we have our continuous experience in which this world incessantly stands before our eyes, as existing without question. But, however much this evidence is prior in itself to all the [other] evidences of life (as turned toward the world) and to all the evidences of all the world sciences (since it is the basis that continually supports them), we soon become doubtful about the extent to which, in this capacity, it can lay claim to being apodictic. And, if we follow up this doubt, it becomes manifest that our experiential evidence of the world lacks also the superiority of being the absolutely primary evidence. Concerning the first point, we note that the universal sensuous experience in whose evidence the world is continuously given to us beforehand is obviously not to be taken forthwith as an apodictic evidence, which, as such, would absolutely exclude both the possibility of eventual doubt whether the world is actual and the possibility of its non-being. Not only can a particular experienced thing suffer devaluation as an illusion of the senses; the whole unitarily surveyable nexus, experienced throughout a period of time, can prove to be an illusion, a coherent dream. We need not take the indicating of these possible and sometimes actual reversals of evidence as a sufficient criticism of the evidence in question and see in it a full proof that, in spite of the continual experiencedness of the world, a non-being of the world is conceivable. We shall retain only this much: that the evidence of world-experience would, at all events, need to be criticized with regard to its validity and range, before it could be used for the purposes of a radical grounding of science, and that therefore we must not take that evidence to be, without question, immediately apodictic. It follows that denying acceptance to all the sciences given us beforehand, treating them as, for us, inadmissible prejudices, is not enough. Their universal basis, the experienced world, must also be deprived of its naïve acceptance. The being of the world, by reason of the evidence of natural experience, must no longer be for us an obvious matter of fact; it too must be for us, henceforth, only an acceptance-phenomenon.

If we maintain this attitude, is any being whatever left us as a basis for judgments, let alone for evidences on which we could establish an all-embracing philosophy and, furthermore, do so apodictically? Is not "the world" the name for the universe of whatever exists? If so, how can we avoid starting *in extenso,* and as our first task, that criticism of world-experience which, a moment ago, we merely indicated? Then, if criticism were to yield the result considered likely in advance, would not our whole philosophical aim be frustrated? But what if the world were, in the end, not at all the absolutely first basis for judgments and a being that is intrinsically prior to the world were the already presupposed basis for the existence of the world?

The Ego Cogito as Transcendental Subjectivity.

At this point, following Descartes, we make the great reversal that, if made in the right manner, leads to transcendental subjectivity: the turn to the *ego cogito* as the ultimate and apodictically certain basis for judgments, the basis on which any radical philosophy must be grounded.

Let us consider. As radically meditating philosophers, we now have neither a science that we accept nor a world that exists for us. Instead of simply existing for us—that is, being accepted naturally by us in our experiential believing in its existence—the world is for us only something that claims being. Moreover, that affects the intramundane existence of all other Egos, so that rightly we should no longer speak communicatively, in the plural. Other men than I, and brute animals, are data of experience for me only by virtue of my sensuous experience of their bodily organisms; and, since the validity of this experience too is called in question, I must not use it. Along with other Egos, naturally, I lose all the formations pertaining to sociality and culture. In short, not just corporeal Nature but the whole concrete surrounding life-world is for me, from now on, only a phenomenon of being, instead of something that is.

But, no matter what the status of this phenomenon's claim to actuality and no matter whether, at some future time, I decide critically that the world exists or that it is an illusion, still this phenomenon itself, as mine, is not nothing but is precisely what makes such critical decisions at all possible and accordingly makes possible whatever has for me sense and validity as "true" being—definitively decided or definitively decide-able being. And besides: If I abstained—as I was free to do and as I did—and still abstain from every believing involved in or founded on sensuous experiencing, so that the being of the experienced world remains unaccepted by me, still this abstaining is what it is; and it exists, together with the whole stream of my experiencing life. Moreover, this life is continually there *for me*. Continually, in respect of a field of the present, it is given to consciousness perceptually, with the most origi-nary originality, as it itself; memorially, now these and now those pasts thereof are "again" given to consciousness, and that implies: as the "pasts themselves". Reflecting, I can at any time look at this original living and note particulars; I can grasp what is present as present, what is past as past, each as itself. I do so now, as the Ego who philosophizes and exercises the aforesaid abstention.

Meanwhile the world experienced in this reflectively grasped life goes on being for me (in a certain manner) "experienced" as before, and with just the content it has at any particular time. It goes on appearing, as it appeared before; the only difference is that I, as reflecting philosophically, no longer keep in effect (no longer accept) the natural believing in existence involved in experiencing the world—though that believing too is still there and grasped by my noticing regard. The same is true of all the processes of meaning that, in addition to the world-experiencing ones, belong to my lifestream: the non-intuitive processes of meaning objects, the judgings, valuings, and decidings, the processes of setting ends and willing means, and all the rest, in particular the position-takings necessarily involved in them all when I am in the natural and non-reflective attitude—since precisely these position-takings always presuppose the world, i.e., involve believing in its existence. Here too the philosophically reflective Ego's abstention from position-takings, his depriving them of acceptance, does not signify their disappearance from his field of experience. The concrete subjective processes, let us repeat, are indeed the things to which his attentive regard is directed: but the attentive Ego, qua philosophizing Ego, practices abstention with respect to what he intuits. Likewise everything *meant* in such accepting or positing processes of consciousness (the meant judgment, theory, value, end, or whatever it is) is still retained completely—but with the acceptance-modification, "mere phenomenon".

This universal depriving of acceptance, this "inhibiting" or "putting out of play" of all positions taken toward the already-given Objective world and, in the first place, all existential positions (those concerning being, illusion, possible being, being likely, probable, etc.),—or, as it is also called, this "phenomenological epoché" and "parenthesizing" of the Objective world—therefore does not leave us confronting nothing. On the contrary we gain possession of something by it; and what we (or, to speak more precisely, what I, the one who is meditating) acquire by it is my pure living, with all the pure subjective processes making this up, and everything meant in them, *purely as* meant in them: the universe of "phenomena" in the (particular and also the wider) phenomenological sense. The epoché can also be said to be the radical and universal method by which I apprehend myself purely: as Ego, and with my own pure conscious life, in and by which the entire Objective world exists for me and is precisely as it is for me. Anything belonging to the world, any spatiotemporal being, exists for me—that is to say, is accepted by me—in that I experience it, perceive it, remember it, think of it somehow, judge about it, value it, desire it, or the like. Descartes, as we know, indicated all that by the name *cogito.* The world is for me absolutely nothing else but the world existing for and accepted by me in such a conscious *cogito.* It gets its whole sense, universal and specific, and its acceptance as existing, exclusively from such *cogitationes.* In these my whole world-life goes on, including my scientifically inquiring and grounding life. By my living, by my experiencing, thinking, valuing, and acting, I can enter no world other than the one that gets its sense and acceptance or status [*Sinn und Geltung*] in and from me, myself. If I put myself above all this life and refrain from doing any believing that takes "the" world straightforwardly as existing—if I direct my regard exclusively to this life itself, as consciousness of "the" world—I thereby acquire myself as the pure ego, with the pure stream of my *cogitationes.*

Thus the being of the pure ego and his *cogitationes,* as a being that is prior in itself, is antecedent to the natural being of the world—the world of which I always speak, the one of which I *can* speak. Natural being is a realm whose existential status [*Seinsgeltung*] is secondary; it continually presupposes the realm of transcendental being. The fundamental phenomenological method of transcendental epoché, because it leads back to this realm, is called transcendental-phenomenological reduction.

9

G. E. Moore,
"Certainty,"
from *Philosophical Papers*

The philosophical method of G. E. Moore (1873–1958) was a patient and detailed scrutiny of problematic concepts. With Bertrand Russell, he is credited with the demolition of the post-Kantian German idealist philosophical tradition of the nineteenth century. Principia Ethica, *1903, became the bible of the "Bloomsbury group," an early twentieth-century circle of artists, writers, and philosophers which included Roger Fry, Virginia Woolf, E. M. Forster, John Maynard Keynes, Clive Bell, and Lytton Strachey. In* Principia Ethica *Moore wrote that "It appears to me that in Ethics, as in all other philosophical studies, the difficulties and disagreements, of which its history is full, are mainly due to a very simple cause: namely to the attempt to answer questions, without first discovering precisely* what *question it is which you desire to answer."*

I am at present, as you can all see, in a room and not in the open air; I am standing up, and not either sitting or lying down; I have clothes on, and am not absolutely naked; I am speaking in a fairly loud voice, and am not either singing or whispering or keeping quite silent; I have in my hand some sheets of paper with writing on them; there are a good many other people in the same room in which I am; and there are windows in that wall and a door in this one.

Now I have here made a number of different assertions; and I have made these assertions quite positively, as if there were no doubt whatever that they were true. That is to say, though I did not expressly say, with regard to any of these different things which I asserted, that it was not only true but also *certain*, yet by asserting them in the way I did, I *implied*, though I did not say, that they were in fact certain— implied, that is, that I myself knew for certain, in each case, that what I asserted to be the case was, at the time when I asserted it, in fact

From G. E. Moore, *Collected Papers*, London, Allen & Unwin, 1959. Reprinted by permission of Timothy Moore and Routledge.

the case. And I do not think that I can be justly accused of dogmatism or over-confidence for having asserted these things positively in the way that I did. In the case of some kinds of assertions, and under some circumstances, a man can be justly accused of dogmatism for asserting something positively. But in the case of assertions such as I made, made under the circumstances under which I made them, the charge would be absurd. On the contrary, I should have been guilty of absurdity if, under the circumstances, I had *not* spoken positively about these things, if I spoke of them at all. Suppose that now, instead of saying 'I am inside a building', I were to say 'I *think* I'm inside a building, but perhaps I'm not: it's not *certain* that I am', or instead of saying 'I have got some clothes on', I were to say 'I think I've got some clothes on, but it's just possible that I haven't.' Would it not sound rather ridiculous for me now, under these circumstances, to say '*I think* I've got some clothes on' or even to say 'I not only think I have, I know that it is very likely indeed that I have, but I can't be quite sure'? For some persons, under some circumstances, it might not be at all absurd to express themselves thus doubtfully. Suppose, for instance, there were a blind man, suffering in addition from general anaesthesia, who knew, because he had been told, that his doctors from time to time stripped him naked and then put his clothes on again, although he himself could neither see nor feel the difference: to such a man there might well come an occasion on which he would really be describing correctly the state of affairs by saying that he *thought* he'd got some clothes on, or that he knew that it was very likely he had, but was not quite sure. But for me, now, in full possession of my senses, it would be quite ridiculous to express myself in this way, because the circumstances are such as to make it quite obvious that I don't merely think that I have, but know that I have. For me now, it would be absurd to say that I *thought* I wasn't naked, because by saying this I should imply that I didn't know that I wasn't, whereas you can all see that I'm in a position to know that I'm not. But if *now* I am not guilty of dogmatism in asserting positively that I'm not naked, certainly I was not guilty of dogmatism when I asserted it positively in one of those sentences with which I began this lecture. I knew then that I had clothes on, just as I know now that I have.

Now those seven assertions with which I began were obviously, in some respects, not all of quite the same kind. For instance: while the first six were all of them (among other things) assertions about myself, the seventh, namely that there were windows in that wall, and a door

in this one, was not about myself at all. And even among those which
were about myself there were obvious differences. In the case of two
of these—the assertions that I was in a room, and the assertion that
there were a good many other people in the same room with me—it
can quite naturally be said that each gave a partial answer to the
question what sort of *environment* I was in at the time when I made
them. And in the case of three others—the assertions that I had clothes
on, that I was speaking in a fairly loud voice, and that I had in my
hand some sheets of paper—it can also be said, though less naturally,
that they each gave a partial answer to the same question. For, if I had
clothes on, if I was in a region in which fairly loud sounds were audible,
and if I had some sheets of paper in my hand, it follows, in each case,
that the surroundings of my body were, in at least one respect, different
from what they would have been if that particular thing had not been
true of me; and the term 'environment' is sometimes so used that any
true statement from which it follows that the surroundings of my body
were different, in any respect, from what they might have been is a
statement which gives *some* information, however little, as to the kind
of environment I was in. But though each of these five assertions can
thus, in a sense, be said to have given, if true, *some* information as to
the nature of my environment at the time when I made it, one of them,
the assertion that I was speaking in a fairly loud voice, did not *only* do
this: it also, if true, gave some information of a very different kind.
For to say that I was speaking in a fairly loud voice was not only to
say that there were audible in my neighbourhood fairly loud sounds,
and sounds of which it was also true that they were words; it was also
to say that some sounds of this sort were *being made by me*—a causal
proposition. As for the sixth of the assertions which I made about
myself—the assertion that I was standing up—that can hardly be said
to have given any information as to the nature of my environment at
the time when I made it: it would be naturally described as giving
information only as to the posture of my body at the time in question.
And as for the two assertions I made which were not about myself at
all—the assertions that there were windows in that wall and a door in
this one—though they were, in a sense, assertions about my environment, since the two walls about which I made them were, in fact, in
my neighborhood at the time; yet in making them I was not expressly
asserting that they were in my neighbourhood (had I been doing so,
they would have been assertions about myself) and what I expressly
asserted was something which might have been true, even if they had

not been in my neighbourhood. In this respect they were unlike my assertion that I was in a room, which could not have been true, unless some walls had been in my neighbourhood. From the proposition that there is a door in that wall it does not follow that that wall is in my neighbourhood; whereas from the proposition that I am in a room, it does follow that a wall is in my neighbourhood.

But in spite of these, and other, differences between those seven or eight different assertions, there are several important respects in which they were all alike.

(1) In the first place: All of those seven or eight different assertions, which I made at the beginning of this lecture, were alike in this respect, namely, that every one of them was an assertion, which, though it wasn't in fact false, yet *might have been false*. For instance, consider the time at which I asserted that I was standing up. It is certainly true that at that very time I *might* have been sitting down, though in fact I wasn't; and if I *had* been sitting down at that time, then my assertion that I was standing up would have been false. Since, therefore, I might have been sitting down at that very time, it follows that my assertion that I was standing up was an assertion which *might have been false*, though it wasn't. And the same is obviously true of all the other assertions I made. At the time when I said I was in a room, I might have been in the open air; at the time when I said I had clothes on, I might have been naked; and so on, in all the other cases.

But from the fact that a given assertion might have been false, it always follows that the negation or contradictory of the proposition asserted is not a self-contradictory proposition. For to say that a given proposition might have been false is equivalent to saying that its negation or contradictory might have been true; and from the fact that a given proposition might have been true, it always follows that the proposition in question is not self-contradictory, since, if it were, it could not possibly have been true. Accordingly all those things which I asserted at the beginning of this lecture were things of which the *contradictories were not self-contradictory*. If, for instance, when I said 'I am standing up' I had said instead 'It is not the case that I am standing up', which would have been the contradictory of what I did say, it would have been correct to say 'That is not a self-contradictory proposition, though it is a false one'; and the same is true in the case of all the other propositions that I asserted. As a short expression for the long expression 'proposition which is not self-contradictory and of which the contradictory is not self-contradictory' philosophers have often used the technical term 'contingent proposition'. Using the term 'contingent' in this sense, we can say, then, that one respect in which all those seven propositions which I asserted at the beginning of this lecture resembled one another was that *they were all of them contingent.*

And before I go on to mention some other respects in which they were all alike, I think I had better now at once say some things about the consequences of this first fact that they were all of them contingent—things which are very relevant to a proper understanding of the use of the word which forms the title of this lecture, the word 'Certainty'.

The first thing I want to say about the consequences of the fact that all those propositions were contingent is this: namely, that from the mere fact that they were all of them contingent, it does not follow that they were not all *known to be true*—nay more, it does not follow, in the case of any particular person whatever, that *that* person did not know them to be true. Some philosophers have in fact suggested that no contingent proposition is ever, as a matter of fact, known to be true. And I am not *now* disputing that suggestion, though I do in fact hold it to be false, and intend, in the course of this lecture, to dispute it. All that I am asserting *now* is that, even if it is a fact that no contingent proposition is ever known to be true, yet in no case does this *follow* from the mere fact that it is contingent. For instance, that I am now standing up is a contingent proposition; but from the mere fact that it is so, from that fact *alone,* it certainly does not *follow* that I do not know that I am standing up. If it is to be shown—as many philosophers think they can show—that I do *not* know now that I am standing up, some other argument must be brought forward for this contention, over and above the mere fact that this proposition is contingent; for from this fact, by itself, it certainly does not *follow* that I don't know that I am standing up. I say that this is certain, and I do not know that anyone would dispute it. But if I were asked to defend my assertion, I do not know that I could give any better defence than merely to say that the conjunctive proposition 'I know that I am at present standing up, and yet the proposition that I am is contingent' is certainly not itself self-contradictory, even if it is false. Is it not obvious that if I say 'I know that I am at present standing up, although the proposition that I am is contingent', I am certainly not contradicting myself, even if I *am* saying something which is false?

The second thing I want to say about the consequences of the fact that all those seven propositions were contingent is something which follows from the first: namely that from the fact that they were contingent it does not follow, in the case of any single one among them, that it was *possible* that the proposition in question was false. To take, for instance, again, the proposition that I was then standing up: from the fact that this proposition was contingent, it does not follow that, if I had said 'It is possible that it is not the case that I am standing up', I should have been saying something true. That this is so follows from my former contention that the contingency of the proposition in question does not entail that it was not known to be true, because one, at least, of the ways in which we use expressions of the form 'It is possible that *p*' is such that the statement in question cannot be true if the person who makes it knows for certain that *p* is false. We very, very often use expressions of the form 'It is possible that *p*' in such a way that by using such an expression we are making an assertion of our own ignorance on a certain point—an assertion namely that we do not *know* that *p* is false. This is certainly one of the very commonest uses of the word 'possible'; it is a use in which what it expresses is often expressed instead by the use of the word 'may'. For instance, if I were to say 'It is possible that Hitler is dead at this moment' this would naturally be understood to mean exactly the same as if I said 'Hitler *may* be dead at this moment'. And is it not quite plain that if I did assert that Hitler *may* be dead at this moment part at least of what I was asserting would be that I personally did not know for certain that he was not dead? Consequently if I were to assert now 'It is possible that I am not standing up' I should naturally be understood to be asserting that I do not know for certain that I am. And hence, if I do know for certain that I am, my assertion that it is possible that I'm not would be false. Since therefore from the fact that 'I am standing up' is a contingent proposition it does not follow that I do not know that I am, it also does not follow from this fact that it is possible that I am *not*. For if from the contingency of this proposition it did follow that it is possible that I am not standing up, it would also follow that I do not know that I *am* standing up: since from 'It is possible that I am not standing up' there follows 'I do not know that I am standing up'; and if *p* entails *q*, and *q* entails *r*, it *follows* that *p* entails *r*. Since, therefore, our *p* ('the proposition "I am standing up" is contingent') does not entail our *r* ('I do not know that I am standing up'), and since our *q* ('It is possible that I am not standing up') *does* entail our *r*, it follows that our *p* does not entail our *q*: that is to say, the fact that the proposition 'I am standing up' is contingent does not entail the consequence that it is possible that it is false that I am standing up. In no case whatever from the mere fact that a proposition *p* is contingent does it *follow* that it is *possible* that *p* is false. But this, of course, is not to deny that it may, *as a matter of fact*, be true of every contingent proposition that it is possible that it is false. This *will* be true, if no contingent proposition is ever known to be true. But even if this is so, it still remains true that from the mere fact that a proposition is contingent it never *follows* that it *may* be false; this remains true because from the mere fact that a proposition is contingent it never follows that it is not known to be true, and never follows, either, in the case of any particular person, that that person does not know it to be true.

In the above paragraph I confined myself to saying that there is at least one common use of expressions of the form 'It is possible that *p*', such that any person who makes such an assertion is asserting that he personally does not know that *p* is false; and hence the only conclusion to which I am so far entitled is that the mere fact that a given proposition *p* is contingent does not entail the consequence that what is expressed by 'it is possible that not-*p*' will be true, *when 'possible' is used in the way in question*. And it may be thought that there is another use of 'possible' such that from '*p* is contingent' there does follow 'it is possible that *p* is false'. The fact is that the expression 'logically possible' has often been used by philosophers in such a way that many might be tempted to think that it is a mere synonym for 'not self-contradictory.' That it is not a mere synonym for this can, I think, be seen from the fact that the expression 'it is not self-contradictory that I am not standing up' is not English at all, whereas the expression 'It is logically possible that I am not standing up' certainly is English, though it may be doubted whether what it expresses is true. If, however, we consider the expression 'the proposition that I am not standing up is not self-contradictory' I think it would not be incorrect to say that the words 'logically possible' are so used that *in this expression* they could be substituted for 'not self-contradictory' without changing the meaning of the whole expression; and that the same is true whatever other proposition you might take instead of the proposition that I am not standing up. If this be so, then it follows that, in the case of any proposition whatever, from the proposition that that proposition is not self-contradictory it will follow that the proposition in question is also logically possible (and *vice versa*); in other words, for any *p*, '*p* is not self-contradictory' entails '*p* is logically possible'. But this being so, it is very natural to think that it follows that you can also take a further step and say truly that, for any *p*, '*p* is not self-contradictory' entails 'It is logically possible that *p*'; for surely from '*p* is logically possible' it must follow that 'it is logically possible that *p*.' Certainly it is very natural to think this; but for all that, I think it is a mistake to think so. To think that '*p* is logically possible' must entail 'It is logically possible that *p*' is certainly a mere mistake which does not do justice to the subtlety of the differences there may be in the way we use language. And I think it is actually a mistake to say that '*p* is not self-contradictory' entails 'It is logically possible that *p*', even though it does entail '*p* is logically possible'. Consider the following facts. 'It is logically possible that I *should have been* sitting down now' certainly does entail 'The proposition that I am sitting down now is not self-contradictory'. But if this latter proposition did entail 'It is logically possible that I *am* sitting down now' then it would follow that 'It is logically possible that I *should have been* sitting down now' entails 'It is logically possible that I *am* sitting down now'. But does it? Certainly it would be quite unnatural for me, who know that I am standing up, to say the latter, whereas it would be quite natural for me to say the former; and I think perhaps we can go further and say that if I said the latter I should be saying something untrue, whereas if I said the former I should be saying something true; just as if I said 'I *might have been* sitting down now', I should be saying something true, whereas if I said 'I *may* be sitting down now', I should be saying something false. In short I think that even the expression 'It is *logically* possible that so-and-so *is* the case' retains the characteristic which we have seen to belong to one ordinary use of the expression 'It is possible that so-and-so *is* the case', namely that it can only be said *with truth* by a person who does not know that the so-and-so in question is *not* the case. If I were to say now 'It is logically possible that I am sitting down' I should be implying that I don't know that I'm not, and therefore implying something which, if I do know that I'm not, is false. I think that perhaps philosophers have not always paid sufficient attention to the possibility that from the mere fact that a given proposition, *p*, is not self-contradictory, it perhaps does not follow that any person whatever can say with truth 'It is logically possible that *p* is true'. In the case of a non-self-contradictory proposition such as the proposition that I am at present sitting down, if there be a person, for instance some friend of mine in England, who does not know that this proposition is false, then, in his case, from the *conjunction* of the fact that the proposition is not self-contradictory with the fact that he does not know it to be false, it does follow that he could say with truth 'It is logically possible that Moore is at present sitting down'; but if there be another person, myself for instance, who does know that the proposition is false, it is by no means clear that from the mere fact that the proposition is not self-contradictory—from the fact *alone*—it follows that *I* can truly say 'It is logically possible that I am at present sitting down'. From the conjunction of the fact that the proposition is logically possible with the fact that I know it to be false, it does follow that I can truly say 'It is logically possible that I *should have been* sitting down at this moment'; but from the fact that I can truly say this, it certainly does not follow that I can *also* truly say 'It is logically possible that I *am* sitting down'; and it is certain that in fact the two are incompatible: that, if I can truly say 'It is logically possible that I *should have been* sitting down now' then it follows that I *cannot* truly say 'It is logically possible that I *am* sitting down now'. Perhaps, however, our use of the expression 'It is logically possible that so-and-so *is* the case' is not clearly enough fixed to entitle us to say this. What is important is to insist that if 'It is logically possible that *p* is true' is used in such a way that it does follow from '*p* is not self-contradictory', *by itself,* then from 'It is logically possible that *p* is true', it does not follow that *p* is not known to be false. And if a philosopher does choose to use 'It is logically possible that *p* is true' in such an unnatural way as this, there will be a danger that he will sometimes forget that that is the way in which he has chosen to use it, and will fall into the fallacy of thinking that from 'It is logically possible that *p is* true' there *does* follow '*p* is not known to be false'.

The third thing which I wish to say about the consequences of the fact that those seven assertions with which I began this paper were assertions of contingent propositions, is this: that this fact is quite compatible with its being true that every one of those seven things that I asserted was not only true but *absolutely certain.* That this is so again follows from the fact that the mere contingency of a given proposition, *p,* never entails, in the case of any person whatever, that that person does not know *p* to be true. It follows from this fact, because if any person whatever does at a given time know that a given proposition *p* is true, then it follows that that person could say with truth at that time 'It is absolutely certain that *p*'. Thus if I do know now that I am standing up, it follows that I can say with truth 'It is absolutely certain that I am standing up'. Since, therefore, the fact that this proposition is contingent is compatible with its being true that I know that I am standing up, it follows that it must also be compatible with its being true that it is absolutely certain that I am standing up.

I think that possibly some people might be inclined to object to what I have just said on the following ground. I have just said that if a person can ever say with truth, with regard to any particular proposition p, 'I know that p is true', it follows that he can also truly say 'It is absolutely certain that p is true'. But an objector might perhaps say: 'I admit that if a person could ever truly say "I know *with absolute certainty* that p is true" then it would follow that he could also truly say "It *is* absolutely certain that p is true". But what you said was not "know with absolute certainty" but "know"; and surely there must be some difference between "knowing" and "knowing with absolute certainty", since, if there were not, we should never be tempted to use the latter expression. I doubt, therefore, whether a mere "I know that p" does entail "It is absolutely certain that p".' To this objection I should reply: I do not think that the only possible explanation of the fact that we sometimes say 'I know with absolute certainty that so-and-so' and sometimes merely 'I know that so-and-so' is that the latter can be properly used to express something which may be true even when what is expressed by the former is not true: I doubt therefore whether 'I know that p' does not always entail 'I know with absolute certainty that p'. But even if 'I know that p' can be sometimes properly used to express something from which 'I know with absolute certainty that p' does *not* follow, it is certainly also sometimes used in such a way that if I don't know with absolute certainty that p, then it follows that I don't know that p. And I have been and shall be only concerned with uses of 'know' of the latter kind, i.e. with such that 'I know that p' does entail 'I know with absolute certainty that p'. And similarly, even if there are proper uses of the word 'certain', such that a thing can be 'certain' without being 'absolutely certain', there are certainly others (or at least one other) such that if a thing is not absolutely certain it cannot be truly said to be certain; and I have been and shall be concerned only with uses of 'certain' of this latter kind.

Another comment which might be made upon what I have said is that, even if there is *one* use of 'absolutely certain' such that, as I said, it is never logically impossible that a contingent proposition should be absolutely certain, yet there is another use of 'absolutely certain' such that this *is* logically impossible—a sense of 'absolutely certain', that is to say, in which only propositions whose contradictories are self-contradictory can be absolutely certain. Propositions whose contradictories are self-contradictory have sometimes been called 'necessary truths', sometimes 'a priori propositions', sometimes 'tautologies'; and it is sometimes held that the sense in which such propositions can be 'certain', and therefore also the sense in which they can be 'known to be true', must be different from the sense (if any) in which contingent propositions are sometimes 'certain' and 'known to be true'. That this may be so, I do not wish to deny. So far as I can see, it may be the case that, if I say, 'I know that' or 'It is certain that' 'it is not the case that there are any triangular figures which are not trilateral', or 'I know that' or 'It is certain that' 'it is not the case that there are any human beings who are daughters and yet are not female', I am using 'know that' and 'it is certain that' in a different sense from that in which I use them if I say 'I know that' or 'It is certain that' 'I have some clothes on'; and it may be the case that only necessary truths can be known or be certain in the former sense. Accordingly, my statements that from the fact that a given proposition, p, is contingent it does not follow that p is not known and is not certain, should be understood to mean only that there is at least one sense in which 'known' and 'certain' can be properly used, such that this does not follow; just as all that I asserted positively before about the phrase 'It is possible that' was that there is at least one sense in which this phrase can be properly used, such that 'p is contingent' does not entail 'It is possible that p is false'.

Finally, there is one slightly puzzling point about our use of the phrases 'it is possible that' and 'it is certain that', which might lead some people to suspect that some of the things I have been saying about the consequences which follow from the fact that a given proposition is contingent are false, and which therefore I think I had better try to clear up at once.

There are four main types of expression in which the word 'certain' is commonly used. We may say 'I feel certain that . . .', or we may say 'I am certain that . . .', or we may say 'I know for certain that . . .', or finally we may say 'It *is* certain that . . .'. And if we compare the first of these expressions with the two last, it is, of course, very obvious, and has been pointed out again and again, that whereas 'I feel certain that p' may quite well be true in a case in which p is not true—in other words that from the mere fact that I feel certain that so-and-so is the case it never follows that so-and-so is in fact the case—there is at least one common use of 'I know for certain that p' and 'It is certain that p' such that these things can't be true unless p is true. This difference may be brought out by the fact that, e.g., 'I felt certain that he would come, but in fact he didn't' is quite clearly not self-contradictory; it is quite clearly logically possible that I should have felt certain that he would come and that yet he didn't; while, on the other hand, 'I knew for certain that he would come, but he didn't' or 'It was certain that he would come but he didn't' are, for at least one common use of those phrases, self-contradictory: the fact that he didn't come *proves* that I didn't *know* he would come, and that it wasn't certain that he would, whereas it does not prove that I didn't *feel* certain that he would. In other words, 'I feel certain that p' does not *entail* that p is true (although by saying that I feel certain that p, I do *imply* that p is true), but 'I know that p' and 'It is certain that p' do entail that p is true; they can't be true, unless it is. As for the fourth expression 'I *am* certain that . . .' or 'I am quite sure that . . .' (it is perhaps worth noting that in the expressions 'I feel certain that . . .' and 'I am certain that . . .' the word 'sure' or the words 'quite sure' can be substituted for the word 'certain' without change of meaning, whereas in the expressions 'I know for certain that . . .' or 'it is certain that . . .' this is not the case) these expressions are, I think, particularly liable to give rise to fallacious reasoning in philosophical discussions about certainty, because, so far as I can see, they are sometimes used to mean the same as 'I feel certain that . . .' and sometimes, on the contrary, to mean the same as 'I know for certain that'. For instance, the expression 'I was quite sure that he would come, but yet he didn't' *can*, it seems to me, be naturally used in such a way that it is not self-contradictory— which can only be the case if it is in that case merely another way of saying 'I felt quite sure that he would come . . .'; but if on the other hand a philosopher were to say to me now (as many would say) 'You can't be quite sure that you are standing up', he would certainly not be asserting that I can't *feel* certain that I am—a thing which he would not at all wish to dispute—and he certainly would be asserting that, even if I do feel certain that I am, I don't or can't *know for certain* that I am.

There is, therefore, a clear difference in meaning between 'I feel certain that . . .' on the one hand, and 'I know for certain that . . .' or 'It is certain that . . .' on the other. But the point with which I am at present concerned is whether there is not also a difference of importance between each of these expressions 'I feel certain that . . .', 'I am certain that . . .', and 'I know for certain that . . .', on the one hand, and 'It *is* certain that . . .' on the other. The first three expressions are

obviously, in spite of the important difference I have just pointed out
between the first and the last of them, alike in one important respect—
a respect which may be expressed by saying that their meaning is
relative to the person who uses them. They are alike in this respect,
because they all contain the word 'I'. In the case of every sentence
which contains this word, its meaning obviously depends on who it is
that says that sentence; if I say 'I am hot', what I assert by saying this
is obviously something different from what any other person would be
asserting by saying exactly the same words; and it is obvious that what
I assert by saying so may quite well be true even though what another
person asserts by saying exactly the same words at exactly the same
time is false. 'I am hot' said by me at a given time, does not contradict
'I am not hot' said by you at exactly the same time: both may perfectly
well be true. And in the same way, if I say 'I feel certain that there
are windows in that wall' or 'I know for certain that there are windows',
I, by saying this, am making an assertion different from, and logically
independent of, what another person would be asserting by saying
exactly the same words at the same time: from the fact that I feel
certain of or know for certain a given thing it *never* follows, in the case
of any other person whatever, that he feels certain of or knows the
thing in question, nor from the fact that he does does it ever follow
that *I* do. But if we consider, by contrast, the expression 'It *is* certain
that there are windows in that wall', it looks, at first sight, as if the
meaning of this expression was *not* relative to the person who says it:
as if it were a quite impersonal statement and should mean the same
whoever says it, provided it is said at the same time and provided the
wall referred to by the words 'that wall' is the same. It is, indeed,
obvious, I think, that a thing can't be certain, unless it is *known:* this
is one obvious point that distinguishes the use of the word 'certain'
from that of the word 'true'; a thing that nobody knows may quite well
be true, but cannot possibly be certain. We can, then, say that it is a
necessary condition for the truth of 'It is certain that *p*' that somebody
should know that *p* is true. But the meaning of 'Somebody knows that
p is true' is certainly not relative to the person who says it: it is as
completely impersonal as 'The sun is larger than the moon', and if
two people say it at the same time, then, if the one by saying it is saying
something true, so must the other be. If, therefore, 'It is certain that
p' meant merely 'Somebody knows that *p* is true', then the meaning
of 'It is certain that *p*' would *not* be relative to the person who says it,
and there would then be an important difference between it, on the

one hand, and 'I feel certain that p' or 'I know for certain that p' on the other, since the meaning of these two *is* relative to the person who says them. But though 'Somebody knows that p is true' is a necessary condition for the truth of 'It is certain that p', it can be easily seen that it is *not* a sufficient condition; for if it were, it would follow that in any case in which somebody did know that p was true, it would always be false for anybody to say 'It is not certain that p'. But in fact it is quite evident that if I say now 'It is not certain that Hitler is still alive', I am not thereby committing myself to the statement that nobody knows that Hitler is still alive: my statement is quite consistent with its being true that Hitler is still alive, and that he himself and other persons know that he is so. The fact is, then, that all that follows from 'Somebody knows that p is true' is that *somebody* could say with truth 'It is certain that p': it does not follow that more than one person could; nor does it follow that there are not some who could say with truth 'It is *not* certain that p'. Two different people, who say, at the same time about the same proposition, p, the one 'It is certain that p is true', the other 'It is not certain that p is true', may both be saying what is true and not contradicting one another. It follows, therefore, that, in spite of appearances, the meaning of 'It *is* certain that p' is relative to the person who says it. And this, I think, is because, as I have implied above, if anybody asserts 'It is certain that p' part of what he is asserting is that he himself knows that p is true; so that, even if many other people do know that p is true, yet his assertion will be false, if he himself does not know it. If, on the other hand, a person asserts 'It is *not* certain that p' his assertion will not necessarily be true merely because he personally does not know that p is true, though it will necessarily be false if he personally does know that p is true. If *I* say 'It is certain that p', that *I* should know that p is true is both a necessary and sufficient condition for the truth of my assertion. But if I say 'It is *not* certain that p', then that I should *not* know that p is true, though it is a necessary, is not a sufficient condition for the truth of my assertion. And similarly the expression 'It is possible that p is true' is, though it looks as if it were impersonal, really an expression whose meaning is relative to the person who uses it. If *I* say it, that I should not know that p is false, is a necessary, though not a sufficient, condition for the truth of my assertion; and hence if two people say it at the same time about the same proposition it is perfectly possible that what the one asserts should be true, and what the other asserts false: since, if one of the two knows that p is false, his assertion will necessarily be false;

whereas, if the other does not know that p is false, his assertion may be, though it will not necessarily be, true. On the other hand, if it were right to use the expression 'It is *logically* possible that p' as equivalent to 'p is not self-contradictory', then the meaning of 'It is *logically* possible that p' would *not* be relative to the person who says it.

To sum up this digression. What I have said about the consequences of the fact that all those seven propositions with which I opened this lecture were contingent, is firstly (1) that this fact does *not* entail the consequence that I did not, when I made them, know them to be true; (2) that it does *not* entail the consequence that I could then have said with truth about any of them 'It is possible that this is false'; and (3) that it does not entail the consequence that I could then have said with truth about any of them 'It is not absolutely certain that this is true'. It follows that by asserting that those seven propositions were contingent, I have not committed myself to the view that they were not known to be true or that it was not absolutely certain they were. But on the other hand, even if I am right in saying that these consequences do *not* follow from the mere fact that they were contingent, it, of course, does not follow from this that I *did* know them to be true, when I asserted them, or that they were absolutely certain. The questions whether, when I first said that I was standing up, I did know that I was, and whether, therefore, it was absolutely certain that I was, still remain completely open.

(2) A second respect, in addition to the fact that they were all of them contingent, in which all those seven propositions resembled one another, was this: In the case of every one of them part at least of what I was asserting, in asserting it, was something from which nothing whatever about the state or condition of my own mind followed— something from which no psychological proposition whatever about myself followed. Every one of them asserted something which might have been true, no matter what the condition of my mind had been either at that moment or in the past. For instance, that I was then inside a room is something which might have been true, even if at the time I had been asleep and in a dreamless sleep, and no matter what my character or disposition or mental abilities might have been: from that fact alone no psychological proposition whatever about myself followed. And the same is true of part at least of what I asserted in each of the other six propositions. I am going to refer to this common feature of all those seven propositions, by saying that they were all of them propositions which implied the existence of *an external world*—

that is to say, of a world *external to my mind*. These phrases 'external world' and 'external to my mind' have often been used in philosophy; and I think that the way in which I am now proposing to use them is in harmony with the way in which they generally (though not always) have been used. It is indeed not obvious that my assertion that I was standing up implied the existence of anything external to *my body;* but it has generally been clear that those who spoke of a world *external* to any given individual, meant by that a world external to that individual's *mind,* and that they were using the expression 'external to a mind' in some metaphorical sense such that my body *must* be external to my mind. Accordingly a proposition which implies the existence of my body does, for that reason alone, with this use of terminology, imply the existence of a world *external to my mind;* and I think that the reason why it is said to do so is because from the existence of my body at a given time nothing whatever logically follows as to the state or condition of my mind at that time. I think, therefore, that I am not saying anything that will be misleading to those familiar with philosophical terminology, if I say, for the reason given, that each of those seven assertions implied the existence of something external to my mind; and that hence, if I did know any one of them to be true, when I asserted it, the existence of an external world was at that time absolutely certain. If, on the other hand, as some philosophers have maintained, the existence of an external world is never absolutely certain, then it follows that I cannot have known any one of these seven propositions to be true.

(3) A third characteristic which was common to all those seven propositions was one which I am going to express by saying that I had for each of them, at the time when I made it, *the evidence of my senses.* I do not mean by this that the evidence of my senses was the *only* evidence I had for them: I do not think it was. What I mean is that, at the time when I made each, I was seeing or hearing or feeling things (or, if that will make my meaning clearer, 'having visual, auditory, tactile or organic sensations'), or a combination of these, such that to see or hear or feel those things *was* to have evidence (not necessarily *conclusive* evidence) for part at least of what I asserted when I asserted the proposition in question. In other words, in all seven cases, what I said was at least partly *based* on 'the then present evidence of my senses'.

(4) Fourth and finally, I think that all those seven assertions shared in common the following characteristic. Consider the class of all propositions which resemble them in the second respect I mentioned, namely,

that they imply the existence of something external to the mind of the person who makes them. It has been and still is held by many philosophers that no proposition which has this peculiarity is ever known to be true—is ever quite certain. And what I think is true of those seven propositions with which I began this lecture is this: namely, that, if I did not know them to be true when I made them, then those philosophers are right. That is to say, if those propositions were not certain, then nothing of the kind is ever certain: if *they* were not certain, then no proposition which implies the existence of anything external to the mind of the person who makes it is ever certain. Take any one of the seven you like: the case for saying that I *knew* that one to be true when I made it is as strong as the case ever is for saying of any proposition which implies the existence of something external to the mind of the person who makes it, that *that* person knows it to be true.

This, it will be seen, is not a matter of logic. Obviously it is logically possible, for instance, that it should have been false then that I knew I was standing up and yet should be true now that I know I am standing up. And similarly in the other cases. But though this is logically possible—though the proposition 'I know that I am standing up now, but I did not know then that I was' is certainly not self-contradictory— yet it seems to me that it is certainly false. If I didn't know then that I was standing up, then certainly I know nothing of the sort now, and never have known anything of the sort; and, not only so, but nobody else ever has. And similarly, conversely (though this also is not a matter of logic), if I did know then that I was standing up then I certainly also know that I am standing up now, and have in the past constantly known things of the sort; and, not only so, but millions of other people have constantly known things of the sort: we all of us constantly do. In other words, those seven propositions of mine seem to be as good test-cases as could have been chosen (*as* good as, but also no better than thousands of others) for deciding between what seems to me to be the only real (though far from the only logically possible) alternatives— namely the alternative that none of us ever knows for certain of the existence of anything external to his own mind, and the alternative that all of us—millions of us—constantly do. And it was because they seemed to me to be as good test-cases as could be chosen for deciding this that I chose them.

But can we decide between these two alternatives?

I feel that the discussion of this question is frightfully difficult; and I feel sure that better and more decisive things could be said about it than I shall be able to say. All that I can do is to discuss, and that very inadequately, just one of the types of argument which have sometimes been alleged to show that nobody ever has known for certain anything about a world external to his mind.

Suppose I say now: 'I know for certain that I am standing up; it is absolutely certain that I am; there is not the smallest chance that I am not.' Many philosophers would say: 'You are wrong: you do not know that you are standing up; it is *not* absolutely certain that you are; there is *some* chance, though perhaps only a very small one, that you are not.' And one argument which has been used as an argument in favour of saying this, is an argument in the course of which the philosopher who used it would assert: 'You do not know for certain that you are not dreaming; it is not absolutely certain that you are not; there is *some* chance, though perhaps only a very small one, that you are.' And from this, that I do not know for certain that I am not dreaming, it is supposed to follow that I do not know for certain that I am standing up. It is argued: If it is not certain that you are not dreaming, then it is not certain that you are standing up. And that *if* I don't know that I'm not dreaming, I also don't know that I'm not sitting down, I don't feel at all inclined to dispute. From the hypothesis that I am dreaming, it would, I think, certainly follow that I don't *know* that I am standing up; though I have never seen the matter argued, and though it is not at all clear to me how it is to be proved that it would follow. But, on the other hand, from the hypothesis that I am dreaming, it certainly would not follow that I am *not* standing up; for it is certainly logically possible that a man should be fast asleep and dreaming, while he is standing up and not lying down. It is therefore logically possible that I should both be standing up and also at the same time dreaming that I am; just as the story, about a well-known Duke of Devonshire, that he once dreamt that he was speaking in the House of Lords and, when he woke up, found that he *was* speaking in the House of Lords, is certainly logically possible. And if, as is commonly assumed, when I am dreaming that I am standing up it may also be correct to say that I am *thinking* that I am standing up, then it follows that the hypothesis that I am now dreaming is quite consistent with the hypothesis that I am both thinking that I am standing up and also actually standing up. And hence, if, as seems to me to be certainly the case and as this argument assumes, from the hypothesis that I am now dreaming it *would* follow that I don't know that I am standing up, there follows a point which is of great importance with regard to our use of the word

'knowledge', and therefore also of the word 'certainty'—a point which
has been made quite conclusively more than once by Russell, namely
that from the conjunction of the two facts that a man thinks that a
given proposition p is true, and that p is in fact true, it does *not* follow
that the man in question *knows* that p is true: in order that I may be
justified in saying that I know that I am standing up, something more
is required than the mere conjunction of the two facts that I both think
I am and actually am—as Russell has expressed it, true belief is not
identical with knowledge; and I think we may further add that even
from the conjunction of the two facts that I feel certain that I am and
that I actually am it would not follow that I know that I am, nor therefore
that it *is* certain that I am. As regards the argument drawn from the
fact that a man who dreams that he is standing up and happens at the
moment actually to be standing up will nevertheless not *know* that he
is standing up, it should indeed be noted that from the fact that a man
is dreaming that he is standing up, it certainly does not *follow* that he
thinks he is standing up; since it does sometimes happen in a dream
that we *think* that it is a dream, and a man who thought this certainly
might, although he was dreaming that he was standing up, yet *think*
that he was not, although he could not *know* that he was not. It is not
therefore the case, as might be hastily assumed, that, if I dream that
I am standing up at a time when I am in fact lying down, I am necessarily
deceived: I should be deceived only if I thought I was standing when I
wasn't; and I may dream that I am, without thinking that I am. It
certainly does, however, often happen that we do dream that so-and-
so is the case, without at the time thinking that we are only dreaming;
and in such cases, I think we may perhaps be said to *think* that what
we dream is the case *is* the case, and to be deceived if it is not the
case; and therefore also, in such cases, if what we dream to be the
case happens also to *be* the case, we may be said to be thinking truly
that it is the case, although we certainly do not *know* that it is.

I agree, therefore, with that part of this argument which asserts that
if I don't know now that I'm not dreaming, it follows that I don't *know*
that I am standing up, even if I both actually am and think that I am.
But this first part of the argument is a consideration which cuts both
ways. For, if it is true, it follows that it is also true that if I *do* know
that I am standing up, then I do know that I am not dreaming. I can
therefore just as well argue: since I do know that I'm standing up, it
follows that I do know that I'm not dreaming; as my opponent can
argue: since you don't know that you're not dreaming, it follows that

you don't know that you're standing up. The one argument is just as good as the other, unless my opponent can give better reasons for asserting that I don't know that I'm not dreaming, than I can give for asserting that I do know that I am standing up.

What reasons can be given for saying that I don't know for certain that I'm not at this moment dreaming?

I do not think that I have ever seen clearly stated any argument which is supposed to show this. But I am going to try to state, as clearly as I can, the premisses and the reasonings from them, which I think have led so many philosophers to suppose that I really cannot now know for certain that I am not dreaming.

I said, you may remember, in talking of the seven assertions with which I opened this lecture, that I had 'the evidence of my senses' for them, though I also said that I didn't think this was the only evidence I had for them, nor that this by itself was necessarily conclusive evidence. Now if I had *then* 'the evidence of my senses' in favour of the proposition that I was standing up, I certainly have *now* the evidence of my senses in favour of the proposition that I *am* standing up, even though this may not be all the evidence that I have, and may not be conclusive. But have I, in fact, the evidence of my senses *at all* in favour of this proposition? One thing seems to me to be quite clear about our use of this phrase, namely, that, if a man at a given time is only dreaming that he is standing up, then it follows that he has *not* at that time the evidence of his senses in favour of that proposition: to say 'Jones last night was *only* dreaming that he was standing up, and yet all the time he had the evidence of his senses that he was' is to say something self-contradictory. But those philosophers who say it is possible that I am now dreaming, certainly mean to say also that it is possible that I am *only dreaming* that I am standing up; and this view, we now see, entails that it is possible that I have *not* the evidence of my senses that I am. If, therefore, they are right, it follows that it is not certain even that I have the evidence of my senses that I am; it follows that it is not certain that I have *the evidence of my senses* for anything at all. If, therefore, I were to say now, that I certainly have the evidence of my senses in favour of the proposition that I am standing up, even if it's not certain that I am standing up, I should be begging the very question now at issue. For if it is not certain that I am not dreaming, it is not certain that I even have the evidence of my senses that I am standing up.

But, now, even if it is not certain that I have at this moment the evidence of my senses for anything at all, it is quite certain that I *either* have the evidence of my senses that I am standing up *or* have an experience which is *very like* having the evidence of my senses that I am standing up. *If* I am dreaming, this experience consists in having dream-images which are at least very like the sensations I should be having if I were awake and had the sensations, the having of which would constitute 'having the evidence of my senses' that I am standing up. Let us use the expression 'sensory experience', in such a way that this experience which I certainly am having will be a 'sensory experience', whether or not it merely consists in the having of dream-images. If we use the expression 'sensory experience' in this way, we can say, I think, that, if it is not certain that I am not dreaming now, then it is not certain that *all* the sensory experiences I am now having are not mere dream-images.

What then are the premisses and the reasonings which would lead so many philosophers to think that all the sensory experiences I am having now *may* be mere dream-images—that I do not know for certain that they are not?

So far as I can see, one premiss which they would certainly use would be this: 'Some at least of the sensory experiences which you are having now are similar in important respects to dream-images which actually have occurred in dreams.' This seems a very harmless premiss, and I am quite willing to admit that it is true. But I think there is a very serious objection to the procedure of using it as a premiss in favour of the derived conclusion. For a philosopher who does use it as a premiss, is, I think, in fact *implying*, though he does not expressly say, that he himself knows it to be true. He is *implying* therefore that he himself knows that dreams have occurred. And, of course, I think he would be right. All the philosophers I have ever met or heard of certainly did know that dreams have occurred: we all know that dreams *have* occurred. But can he consistently combine this proposition that he knows that dreams have occurred, with his conclusion that he does not know that he is not dreaming? Can anybody possibly know that dreams have occurred, if, at the time, he does not himself know that he is not dreaming? If he *is* dreaming, it may be that he is only dreaming that dreams have occurred; and if he does not know that he is not dreaming, can he possibly know that he is *not* only dreaming that dreams have occurred? Can he possibly know therefore that dreams *have* occurred? I do not think that he can; and therefore I think that anyone who uses this premiss and also asserts the conclusion that nobody ever knows he is not dreaming, is guilty of an inconsistency. By using this premiss he implies that he himself knows that dreams have occurred; while, if his conclusion is true, it follows that he himself does not know that he is not dreaming, and therefore does not know that he is not only dreaming that dreams have occurred.

However, I admit that the premiss is true. Let us now try to see by what sort of reasoning it might be thought that we could get from it to the conclusion.

I do not see how we can get forward in that direction at all, unless we first take the following huge step, unless we say, namely: since there have been dream-images similar in important respects to some of the sensory experiences I am now having, it is logically possible that there should be dream-images *exactly like all* the sensory experiences I am now having, and logically possible, therefore, that all the sensory experiences I am now having *are* mere dream-images. And it might be thought that the validity of this step could be supported to some extent by appeal to matters of fact, though only, of course, at the cost of the same sort of inconsistency which I have just pointed out. It might be said, for instance, that some people have had dream-images which were *exactly like* sensory experiences which they had when they were awake, and that therefore it must be logically possible to have a dream-image exactly like a sensory experience which is *not* a dream-image. And then it may be said: If it is logically possible for some dream-images to be exactly like sensory experiences which are not dream-images, surely it must be logically possible for *all* the dream-images occurring in a dream at a given time to be exactly like sensory experiences which are not dream-images, and logically possible also for all the sensory experiences which a man has at a given time when he is awake to be exactly like all the dream-images which he himself or another man had in a dream at another time.

Now I cannot see my way to deny that it is logically possible that all the sensory experiences I am having now should be mere dream-images. And if this is logically possible, and if further the sensory experiences I am having now were the only experiences I am having, I do not see how I could possibly know for certain that I am not dreaming.

But the conjunction of my memories of the immediate past with these sensory experiences *may* be sufficient to enable me to know that I am not dreaming. I say it *may* be. But what if our sceptical philosopher says: It is *not* sufficient; and offers as an argument to prove that it is not, this: It is logically possible *both* that you should be having all the sensory experiences you are having, and also that you should be remembering what you do remember, and *yet* should be dreaming. If this *is* logically possible, then I don't see how to deny that I cannot possibly know for certain that I am not dreaming: I do not see that I possibly could. But can any reason be given for saying that it *is* logically possible? So far as I know nobody ever has, and I don't know how anybody ever could. And so long as this is not done my argument, 'I know that I am standing up, and therefore I know that I am not dreaming', remains at least as good as his, 'You don't know that you are not dreaming, and therefore don't know that you are standing up'. And I don't think I've ever seen an argument expressly directed to show that it is not.

One final point should be made clear. It is certainly logically possible that I *should have* been dreaming now; I *might* have been dreaming now; and therefore the proposition that I *am* dreaming now is not self-contradictory. But what I am in doubt of is whether it is logically possible that I should *both* be having all the sensory experiences and the memories that I have and *yet* be dreaming. The conjunction of the proposition that I have these sense experiences and memories with the proposition that I am dreaming does seem to me to be very likely self-contradictory.[1]

---

1 According to Casimir Lewy, Moore's editor, Moore was particularly dissatis-fied with the last paragraphs of "Certainty". The original manuscript is now in the Cambridge University Library. Moore deleted the last five paragraphs of his original ending, substituting the ones given above. For the deleted version, see G. E. Moore, *Selected Writings*, ed. Thomas Baldwin, London, Routledge, 1993, pp. 195–96.

10

Ludwig Wittgenstein, "On Certainty," from *On Certainty*

Ludwig Wittgenstein (1889–1951), the author of the Tractatus Logico-Philosophicus *of 1921 and the posthumously published* Philosophical Investigations *of 1953, is thought by many to be the greatest philosopher of the twentieth century.* On Certainty *was written shortly before his death in 1951.*

1. If you do know that *here is one hand,*[1] we'll grant you all the rest.

When one says that such and such a proposition can't be proved, of course that does not mean that it can't be derived from other propositions; any proposition can be derived from other ones. But they may be no more certain than it is itself. (On this a curious remark by H. Newman.)

2. From its *seeming* to me—or to everyone—to be so, it doesn't follow that it *is* so.

What we can ask is whether it can make sense to doubt it.

3. If e.g. someone says "I don't know if there's a hand here" he might be told "Look closer".—This possibility of satisfying oneself is part of the language-game. Is one of its essential features.

4. "I know that I am a human being." In order to see how unclear the sense of this proposition is, consider its negation. At most it might

From L. Wittgenstein, *On Certainty*, edited by G. E. M. Anscombe and G. H. von Wright, Oxford, Blackwell, 1969.

1. See G. E. Moore, "Proof of an External World", *Proceedings of the British Academy*, Vol. XXV, 1939; also "A Defence of Common Sense" in *Contemporary British Philosophy, 2nd Series*, Ed. J. H. Muirhead, 1925. Both papers are in Moore's *Philosophical Papers*, London, George Allen and Unwin, 1959. *Editors.*

be taken to mean "I know I have the organs of a human". (E.g. a brain, which, after all, no one has ever yet seen.) But what about such a proposition as "I know I have a brain"? Can I doubt it? Grounds for *doubt* are lacking! Everything speaks in its favour, nothing against it. Nevertheless it is imaginable that my skull should turn out empty when it was operated on.

5. Whether a proposition can turn out false after all depends on what I make count as determinants for that proposition.

6. Now, can one enumerate what one knows (like Moore)? Straight off like that, I believe not.—For otherwise the expression "I know" gets misused. And through this misuse a queer and extremely important mental state seems to be revealed.

7. My life shews that I know or am certain that there is a chair over there, or a door, and so on.—I tell a friend e.g. "Take that chair over there", "Shut the door", etc. etc.

8. The difference between the concept of 'knowing' and the concept of 'being certain' isn't of any great importance at all, except where "I know" is meant to mean: I *can't* be wrong. In a law-court, for example, "I am certain" could replace "I know" in every piece of testimony. We might even imagine its being forbidden to say "I know" there. [A passage in *Wilhelm Meister*, where "You know" or "You knew" is used in the sense "You were certain", the facts being different from what he knew.]

9. Now do I, in the course of my life, make sure I know that here is a hand—my own hand, that is?

10. I know that a sick man is lying here? Nonsense! I am sitting at his bedside, I am looking attentively into his face.—So I don't know, then, that there is a sick man lying here? Neither the question nor the assertion makes sense. Any more than the assertion "I am here", which I might yet use at any moment, if suitable occasion presented itself.— Then is "$2 \times 2 = 4$" nonsense in the same way, and not a proposition of arithmetic, apart from particular occasions? "$2 \times 2 = 4$" is a true proposition of arithmetic—not "on particular occasions" nor "always"—but the spoken or written sentence "$2 \times 2 = 4$" in Chinese

might have a different meaning or be out and out nonsense, and from this is seen that it is only in use that the proposition has its sense. And "I know that there's a sick man lying here", used in an *unsuitable* situation, seems not to be nonsense but rather seems matter-of-course, only because one can fairly easily imagine a situation to fit it, and one thinks that the words "I know that . . . " are always in place where there is no doubt, and hence even where the expression of doubt would be unintelligible.

11. We just do not see how very specialized the use of "I know" is.

12. —For "I know" seems to describe a state of affairs which guarantees what is known, guarantees it as a fact. One always forgets the expression "I thought I knew".

13. For it is not as though the proposition "It is so" could be inferred from someone else's utterance: "I know it is so". Nor from the utterance together with its not being a lie.—But can't I infer "It is so" from my own utterance "I know etc."? Yes; and also "There is a hand there" follows from the proposition "He knows that there's a hand there". But from his utterance "I know . . . " it does not follow that he does know it.

14. That he does know takes some shewing.

15. It needs to be *shown* that no mistake was possible. Giving the assurance "I know" doesn't suffice. For it is after all only an assurance that I can't be making a mistake, and it needs to be *objectively* established that I am not making a mistake about *that*.

16. "If I know something, then I also know that I know it, etc." amounts to: "I know that" means "I am incapable of being wrong about that". But whether I am so needs to be established objectively.

17. Suppose now I say "I'm incapable of being wrong about this: that is a book" while I point to an object. What would a mistake here be like? And have I any *clear* idea of it?

18. "I know" often means: I have the proper grounds for my statement. So if the other person is acquainted with the language-game,

he would admit that I know. The other, if he is acquainted with the language-game, must be able to imagine *how* one may know something of the kind.

19. The statement "I know that here is a hand" may then be continued: "for it's *my* hand that I'm looking at". Then a reasonable man will not doubt that I know.—Nor will the idealist; rather he will say that he was not dealing with the practical doubt which is being dismissed, but there is a further doubt *behind* that one.—That this is an *illusion* has to be shewn in a different way.

20. "Doubting the existence of the external world" does not mean for example doubting the existence of a planet, which later observations proved to exist.—Or does Moore want to say that knowing that here is his hand is different in kind from knowing the existence of the planet Saturn? Otherwise it would be possible to point out the discovery of the planet Saturn to the doubters and say that its existence has been proved, and hence the existence of the external world as well.

21. Moore's view really comes down to this: the concept 'know' is analogous to the concepts 'believe', 'surmise', 'doubt', 'be convinced' in that the statement "I know . . ." can't be a mistake. And if that *is* so, then there can be an inference from such an utterance to the truth of an assertion. And here the form "I thought I knew" is being overlooked.—But if this latter is inadmissible, then a mistake in the *assertion* must be logically impossible too. And anyone who is acquainted with the language-game must realize this—an assurance from a reliable man that he *knows* cannot contribute anything.

22. It would surely be remarkable if we had to believe the reliable person who says "I can't be wrong"; or who says "I am not wrong".

23. If I don't know whether someone has two hands (say, whether they have been amputated or not) I shall believe his assurance that he has two hands, if he is trustworthy. And if he says he *knows* it, that can only signify to me that he has been able to make sure, and hence that his arms are e.g. not still concealed by coverings and bandages, etc. etc. My believing the trustworthy man stems from my admitting that it is possible for him to make sure. But someone who says that perhaps there are no physical objects makes no such admission.

24. The idealist's question would be something like: "What right have I not to doubt the existence of my hands?" (And to that the answer can't be: I *know* that they exist.) But someone who asks such a question is overlooking the fact that a doubt about existence only works in a language-game. Hence, that we should first have to ask: what would such a doubt be like?, and don't understand this straight off.

25. One may be wrong even about "there being a hand here". Only in particular circumstances is it impossible.—"Even in a calculation one can be wrong—only in certain circumstances one can't."

26. But can it be seen from a *rule* what circumstances logically exclude a mistake in the employment of rules of calculation?

What use is a rule to us here? Mightn't we (in turn) go wrong in applying it?

27. If, however, one wanted to give something like a rule here, then it would contain the expression "in normal circumstances". And we recognize normal circumstances but cannot precisely describe them. At most, we can describe a range of abnormal ones.

28. What is 'learning a rule'?—*This.*

What is 'making a mistake in applying it'?—*This.* And what is pointed to here is something indeterminate.

29. Practice in the use of the rule also shews what is a mistake in its employment.

30. When someone has made sure of something, he says: "Yes, the calculation is right", but he did not infer that from his condition of certainty. One does not infer how things are from one's own certainty.

Certainty is *as it were* a tone of voice in which one declares how things are, but one does not infer from the tone of voice that one is justified.

31. The propositions which one comes back to again and again as if bewitched—these I should like to expunge from philosophical language.

32. It's not a matter of *Moore's* knowing that there's a hand there, but rather we should not understand him if he were to say "Of course I may be wrong about this". We should ask "What is it like to make such a mistake as that?"—e.g. what's it like to discover that it was a mistake?

33. Thus we expunge the sentences that don't get us any further.

34. If someone is taught to calculate, is he also taught that he can rely on a calculation of his teacher's? But these explanations must after all sometime come to an end. Will he also be taught that he can trust his senses—since he is indeed told in many cases that in such and such a special case you *cannot* trust them?—
Rule and exception.

35. But can't it be imagined that there should be no physical objects? I don't know. And yet "There are physical objects" is nonsense. Is it supposed to be an empirical proposition?—
And is *this* an empirical proposition: "There seem to be physical objects"?

36. "A is a physical object" is a piece of instruction which we give only to someone who doesn't yet understand either what "A" means, or what "physical object" means. Thus it is instruction about the use of words, and "physical object" is a logical concept. (Like colour, quantity, . . .) And that is why no such proposition as: "There are physical objects" can be formulated.
Yet we encounter such unsuccessful shots at every turn.

37. But is it an adequate answer to the scepticism of the idealist, or the assurances of the realist, to say that "There are physical objects" is nonsense? For them after all it is not nonsense. It would, however, be an answer to say: this assertion, or its opposite is a misfiring attempt to express what can't be expressed like that. And that it does misfire can be shewn; but that isn't the end of the matter. We need to realize that what presents itself to us as the first expression of a difficulty, or of its solution, may as yet not be correctly expressed at all. Just as one who has a just censure of a picture to make will often at first offer the censure where it does not belong, and an *investigation* is needed in order to find the right point of attack for the critic.

38. Knowledge in mathematics: Here one has to keep on reminding oneself of the unimportance of the 'inner process' or 'state' and ask "Why should it be important? What does it matter to me?" What is interesting is how we *use* mathematical propositions.

39. *This* is how calculation is done, in such circumstances a calculation is *treated* as absolutely reliable, as certainly correct.

40. Upon "I know that here is my hand" there may follow the question "How do you know?" and the answer to that presupposes that *this* can be known in *that* way. So, instead of "I know that here is my hand", one might say "Here is my hand", and then add *how* one knows.

41. "I know where I am feeling pain", "I know that I feel it *here*" is as wrong as "I know that I am in pain". But "I know where you touched my arm" is right.

42. One can say "He believes it, but it isn't so", but not "He knows it, but it isn't so". Does this stem from the difference between the mental states of belief and of knowledge? No.—One may for example call "mental state" what is expressed by tone of voice in speaking, by gestures etc. It would thus be *possible* to speak of a mental state of conviction, and that may be the same whether it is knowledge or false belief. To think that different states must correspond to the words "believe" and "know" would be as if one believed that different people had to correspond to the word "I" and the name "Ludwig", because the concepts are different.

43. What sort of proposition is this: "We *cannot* have miscalculated in $12 \times 12 = 144$"? It must surely be a proposition of logic.—But now, is it not the same, or doesn't it come to the same, as the statement $12 \times 12 = 144$?

44. If you demand a rule from which it follows that there can't have been a miscalculation here, the answer is that we did not learn this through a rule, but by learning to calculate.

45. We got to know the *nature* of calculating by learning to calculate.

46. But then can't it be described how we satisfy ourselves of the reliability of a calculation? O yes! Yet no rule emerges when we do so.—But the most important thing is: The rule is not needed. Nothing is lacking. We do calculate according to a rule, and that is enough.

47. *This* is how one calculates. Calculating is *this*. What we learn at school, for example. Forget this transcendent certainty, which is connected with your concept of spirit.

48. However, out of a host of calculations certain ones might be designated as reliable once for all, others as not yet fixed. And now, is this a *logical* distinction?

49. But remember: even when the calculation is something fixed for me, this is only a decision for a practical purpose.

50. When does one say, I know that . . . × . . . = . . . ? When one has checked the calculation.

51. What sort of proposition is: "What could a mistake here be like!"? It would have to be a logical proposition. But it is a logic that is not used, because what it tells us is not learned through propositions.—It is a logical proposition; for it does describe the conceptual (linguistic) situation.

52. This situation is thus not the same for a proposition like "At this distance from the sun there is a planet" and "Here is a hand" (namely my own hand). The second can't be called a hypothesis. But there isn't a sharp boundary line between them.

53. So one might grant that Moore was right, if he is interpreted like this: a proposition saying that here is a physical object may have the same logical status as one saying that here is a red patch.

54. For it is not true that a mistake merely gets more and more improbable as we pass from the planet to my own hand. No: at some point it has ceased to be conceivable.
This is already suggested by the following: if it were not so, it would

also be conceivable that we should be wrong in *every* statement about physical objects; that any we ever make are mistaken.

55. So is the *hypothesis* possible, that all the things around us don't exist? Would that not be like the hypothesis of our having miscalculated in all our calculations?

56. When one says: "Perhaps this planet doesn't exist and the light-phenomenon arises in some other way", then after all one needs an example of an object which does exist. This doesn't exist,—as *for example* does. . . .

Or are we to say that *certainty* is merely a constructed point to which some things approximate more, some less closely? No. Doubt gradually loses its sense. This language-game just *is* like that.

And everything descriptive of a language-game is part of logic.

57. Now might not "I *know*, I am not just surmising, that here is my hand" be conceived as a proposition of grammar? Hence *not* temporally.—

But in that case isn't it like *this* one: "I know, I am not just surmising, that I am seeing red"?

And isn't the consequence "So there are physical objects" like: "So there are colours"?

58. If "I know etc." is conceived as a grammatical proposition, of course the "I" cannot be important. And it properly means "There is no such thing as a doubt in this case" or "The expression 'I do not know' makes no sense in this case". And of course it follows from this that "I *know*" makes no sense either.

59. "I know" is here a *logical* insight. Only realism can't be proved by means of it.

60. It is wrong to say that the 'hypothesis' that *this* is a bit of paper would be confirmed or disconfirmed by later experience, and that, in "I know that this is a bit of paper," the "I know" either relates to such an hypothesis or to a logical determination.

61. ... A meaning of a word is a kind of employment of it.
For it is what we learn when the word is incorporated into our language.

62. That is why there exists a correspondence between the concepts 'rule' and 'meaning'.

63. If we imagine the facts otherwise than as they are, certain language-games lose some of their importance, while others become important. And in this way there is an alteration—a gradual one—in the use of the vocabulary of a language.

64. Compare the meaning of a word with the 'function' of an official. And 'different meanings' with 'different functions'.

65. When language-games change, then there is a change in concepts, and with the concepts the meanings of words change.

66. I make assertions about reality, assertions which have different degrees of assurance. How does the degree of assurance come out? What consequences has it?
We may be dealing, for example, with the certainty of memory, or again of perception. I may be sure of something, but still know what test might convince me of error. I am e.g. quite sure of the date of a battle, but if I should find a different date in a recognized work of history, I should alter my opinion, and this would not mean I lost all faith in judging.

67. Could we imagine a man who keeps on making mistakes where we regard a mistake as ruled out, and in fact never encounter one?
E.g. he says he lives in such and such a place, is so and so old, comes from such and such a city, and he speaks with the same certainty (giving all the tokens of it) as I do, but he is wrong.
But what is his relation to this error? What am I to suppose?

68. The question is: what is the logician to say here?

69. I should like to say: "If I am wrong about *this*, I have no guarantee that anything I say is true." But others won't say that about me, nor will I say it about other people.

70. For months I have lived at address A, I have read the name of the street and the number of the house countless times, have received countless letters here and given countless people the address. If I am wrong about it, the mistake is hardly less than if I were (wrongly) to believe I was writing Chinese and not German.

71. If my friend were to imagine one day that he had been living for a long time past in such and such a place, etc. etc., I should not call this a *mistake*, but rather a mental disturbance, perhaps a transient one.

72. Not every false belief of this sort is a mistake.

73. But what is the difference between mistake and mental disturbance? Or what is the difference between my treating it as a mistake and my treating it as mental disturbance?

74. Can we say: a *mistake* doesn't only have a cause, it also has a ground? I.e., roughly: when someone makes a mistake, this can be fitted into what he knows aright.

75. Would this be correct: If I merely believed wrongly that there is a table here in front of me, this might still be a mistake; but if I believe wrongly that I have seen this table, or one like it, every day for several months past, and have regularly used it, that isn't a mistake?

76. Naturally, my aim must be to say what statements one would like to make here, but cannot make significantly.

77. Perhaps I shall do a multiplication twice to make sure, or perhaps get someone else to work it over. But shall I work it over again twenty times, or get twenty people to go over it? And is that some sort of negligence? Would the certainty really be greater for being checked twenty times?

78. And can I give a *reason* why it isn't?

79. That I am a man and not a woman can be verified, but if I were to say I was a woman, and then tried to explain the error by saying I hadn't checked the statement, the explanation would not be accepted.

80. The *truth* of my statements is the test of my *understanding* of these statements.

81. That is to say: if I make certain false statements, it becomes uncertain whether I understand them.

82. What counts as an adequate test of a statement belongs to logic. It belongs to the description of the language-game.

83. The *truth* of certain empirical propositions belongs to our frame of reference.

84. Moore says he *knows* that the earth existed long before his birth. And put like that it seems to be a personal statement about him, even if it is in addition a statement about the physical world. Now it is philosophically uninteresting whether Moore knows this or that, but it is interesting that, and how, it can be known. If Moore had informed us that he knew the distance separating certain stars, we might conclude from that that he had made some special investigations, and we shall want to know what these were. But Moore chooses precisely a case in which we all seem to know the same as he, and without being able to say how. I believe e.g. that I know as much about this matter (the existence of the earth) as Moore does, and if he knows that it is as he says, then *I* know it too. For it isn't, either, as if he had arrived at his proposition by pursuing some line of thought which, while it is open to me, I have not in fact pursued.

85. And what goes into someone's knowing this? Knowledge of history, say? He must know what it means to say: the earth has already existed for such and such a length of time. For not *any* intelligent adult must know that. We see men building and demolishing houses, and are led to ask: "How long has this house been here?" But how does one come on the idea of asking this about a mountain, for example? And have all men the notion of the earth as a *body*, which may come into being and pass away? Why shouldn't I think of the earth as flat, but extending without end in every direction (including depth)? But in that case one might still say "I know that this mountain existed long before my birth."—But suppose I met a man who didn't believe that?

86. Suppose I replaced Moore's "I know" by "I am of the unshake-able conviction"?

87. Can't an assertoric sentence, which was capable of functioning as an hypothesis, also be used as a foundation for research and action? I.e. can't it simply be isolated from doubt, though not according to any explicit rule? It simply gets assumed as a truism, never called in question, perhaps not even ever formulated.

88. It may be for example that *all enquiry on our part* is set so as to exempt certain propositions from doubt, if they are ever formulated. They lie apart from the route travelled by enquiry.

89. One would like to say: "Everything speaks for, and nothing against the earth's having existed long before. . . ."
Yet might I not believe the contrary after all? But the question is: What would the practical effects of this belief be?—Perhaps someone says: "That's not the point. A belief is what it is whether it has any practical effects or not." One thinks: It is the same adjustment of the human mind anyway.

90. "I know" has a primitive meaning similar to and related to "I see" ("wissen", "videre"). And "I knew he was in the room, but he wasn't in the room" is like "I saw him in the room, but he wasn't there". "I know" is supposed to express a relation, not between me and the sense of a proposition (like "I believe") but between me and a fact. So that the *fact* is taken into my consciousness. (Here is the reason why one wants to say that nothing that goes on in the outer world is really known, but only what happens in the domain of what are called sense-data.) This would give us a picture of knowing as the perception of an outer event through visual rays which project it as it is into the eye and the consciousness. Only then the question at once arises whether one can be *certain* of this projection. And this picture does indeed show how our *imagination* presents knowledge, but not what lies at the bottom of this presentation.

91. If Moore says he knows the earth existed etc., most of us will grant him that it has existed all that time, and also believe him when he says he is convinced of it. But has he also got the right *ground* for his conviction? For if not, then after all he doesn't *know* (Russell).

92. However, we can ask: May someone have telling grounds for believing that the earth has only existed for a short time, say since his own birth?—Suppose he had always been told that,—would he have any good reason to doubt it? Men have believed that they could make rain; why should not a king be brought up in the belief that the world began with him? And if Moore and this king were to meet and discuss, could Moore really prove his belief to be the right one? I do not say that Moore could not convert the king to his view, but it would be a conversion of a special kind; the king would be brought to look at the world in a different way.

Remember that one is sometimes convinced of the *correctness* of a view by its *simplicity* or *symmetry,* i.e., these are what induce one to go over to this point of view. One then simply says something like: *"That's how it must be."*

93. The propositions presenting what Moore '*knows*' are all of such a kind that it is difficult to imagine *why* anyone should believe the contrary. E.g. the proposition that Moore has spent his whole life in close proximity to the earth.—Once more I can speak of myself here instead of speaking of Moore. What could induce me to believe the opposite? Either a memory, or having been told.—Everything that I have seen or heard gives me the conviction that no man has ever been far from the earth. Nothing in my picture of the world speaks in favour of the opposite.

94. But I did not get my picture of the world by satisfying myself of its correctness; nor do I have it because I am satisfied of its correctness. No: it is the inherited background against which I distinguish between true and false.

95. The propositions describing this world-picture might be part of a kind of mythology. And their role is like that of rules of a game; and the game can be learned purely practically, without learning any explicit rules.

96. It might be imagined that some propositions, of the form of empirical propositions, were hardened and functioned as channels for such empirical propositions as were not hardened but fluid; and that this relation altered with time, in that fluid propositions hardened, and hard ones became fluid.

97. The mythology may change back into a state of flux, the river-bed of thoughts may shift. But I distinguish between the movement of the waters on the river-bed and the shift of the bed itself; though there is not a sharp division of the one from the other.

98. But if someone were to say "So logic too is an empirical science" he would be wrong. Yet this is right: the same proposition may get treated at one time as something to test by experience, at another as a rule of testing.

99. And the bank of that river consists partly of hard rock, subject to no alteration or only to an imperceptible one, partly of sand, which now in one place now in another gets washed away, or deposited.

100. The truths which Moore says he knows, are such as, roughly speaking, all of us know, if he knows them.

101. Such a proposition might be e.g. "My body has never disappeared and reappeared again after an interval."

102. Might I not believe that once, without knowing it, perhaps in a state of unconsciousness, I was taken far away from the earth—that other people even know this, but do not mention it to me? But this would not fit into the rest of my convictions at all. Not that I could describe the system of these convictions. Yet my convictions do form a system, a structure.

103. And now if I were to say "It is my unshakeable conviction that etc.", this means in the present case too that I have not consciously arrived at the conviction by following a particular line of thought, but that it is anchored in all my *questions and answers*, so anchored that I cannot touch it.

104. I am for example also convinced that the sun is not a hole in the vault of heaven.

105. All testing, all confirmation and disconfirmation of a hypothesis takes place already within a system. And this system is not a more or less arbitrary and doubtful point of departure for all our arguments: no, it belongs to the essence of what we call an argument. The system

is not so much the point of departure, as the element in which arguments have their life.

106. Suppose some adult had told a child that he had been on the moon. The child tells me the story, and I say it was only a joke, the man hadn't been on the moon; no one has ever been on the moon; the moon is a long way off and it is impossible to climb up there or fly there.—If now the child insists, saying perhaps there is a way of getting there which I don't know, etc. what reply could I make to him? What reply could I make to the adults of a tribe who believe that people sometimes go to the moon (perhaps that is how they interpret their dreams), and who indeed grant that there are no ordinary means of climbing up to it or flying there?—But a child will not ordinarily stick to such a belief and will soon be convinced by what we tell him seriously.

107. Isn't this altogether like the way one can instruct a child to believe in a God, or that none exists, and it will accordingly be able to produce apparently telling grounds for the one or the other?

108. "But is there then no objective truth? Isn't it true, or false, that someone has been on the moon?" If we are thinking within our system, then it is certain that no one has ever been on the moon. Not merely is nothing of the sort ever seriously reported to us by reasonable people, but our whole system of physics forbids us to believe it. For this demands answers to the questions "How did he overcome the force of gravity?" "How could he live without an atmosphere?" and a thousand others which could not be answered. But suppose that instead of all these answers we met the reply: "We don't know *how* one gets to the moon, but those who get there know at once that they are there; and even you can't explain everything." We should feel ourselves intellectually very distant from someone who said this.

109. "An empirical proposition can be *tested*" (we say). But how? and through what?

110. What *counts* as its test?—"But is this an adequate test? And, if so, must it not be recognizable as such in logic?"—As if giving grounds did not come to an end sometime. But the end is not an ungrounded presupposition: it is an ungrounded way of acting.

111. "I *know* that I have never been on the moon." That sounds quite different in the circumstances which actually hold, to the way it would sound if a good many men had been on the moon, and some perhaps without knowing it. In *this* case one could give grounds for this knowledge. Is there not a relationship here similar to that between the general rule of multiplying and particular multiplications that have been carried out?

I want to say: my not having been on the moon is as sure a thing for me as any grounds I could give for it.

112. And isn't that what Moore wants to say, when he says he *knows* all these things?—But is his knowing it really what is in question, and not rather that some of these propositions must be solid for us?

113. When someone is trying to teach us mathematics, he will not begin by assuring us that he *knows* that a+b = b+a.

114. If you are not certain of any fact, you cannot be certain of the meaning of your words either.

115. If you tried to doubt everything you would not get as far as doubting anything. The game of doubting itself presupposes certainty.

116. Instead of "I know . . .", couldn't Moore have said: "It stands fast for me that . . ."? And further: "It stands fast for me and many others. . . ."

117. Why is it not possible for me to doubt that I have never been on the moon? And how could I try to doubt it?

First and foremost, the supposition that perhaps I have been there would strike me as *idle*. Nothing would follow from it, nothing be explained by it. It would not tie in with anything in my life.

When I say "Nothing speaks for, everything against it," this presupposes a principle of speaking for and against. That is, I must be able to say what *would* speak for it.

118. Now would it be correct to say: So far no one has opened my skull in order to see whether there is a brain inside; but everything speaks for, and nothing against, its being what they would find there?

119. But can it also be said: Everything speaks for, and nothing against the table's still being there when no one sees it? For what does speak for it?

120. But if anyone were to doubt it, how would his doubt come out in practice? And couldn't we peacefully leave him to doubt it, since it makes no difference at all?

121. Can one say: "Where there is no doubt there is no knowledge either"?

122. Doesn't one need grounds for doubt?

123. Wherever I look, I find no ground for doubting that. . . .

124. I want to say: We use judgments as principles of judgment.

125. If a blind man were to ask me "Have you got two hands?" I should not make sure by looking. If I were to have any doubt of it, then I don't know why I should trust my eyes. For why shouldn't I test my *eyes* by looking to find out whether I see my two hands? *What* is to be tested by *what?* (Who decides *what* stands fast?)
And what does it mean to say that such and such stands fast?

126. I am not more certain of the meaning of my words than I am of certain judgments. Can I doubt that this colour is called "blue"?
(My) doubts form a system.

127. For how do I know that someone is in doubt? How do I know that he uses the words "I doubt it" as I do?

128. From a child up I learnt to judge like this. *This is* judging.

129. This is how I learned to judge; *this* I got to know *as* judgment.

130. But isn't it experience that teaches us to judge like *this,* that is to say, that it is correct to judge like this? But how does experience *teach* us, then? *We* may derive it from experience, but experience does not direct us to derive anything from experience. If it is the *ground* of

our judging like this, and not just the cause, still we do not have a ground for seeing this in turn as a ground.

131. No, experience is not the ground for our game of judging. Nor is its outstanding success.

132. Men have judged that a king can make rain; *we* say this contradicts all experience. Today they judge that aeroplanes and the radio etc. are means for the closer contact of peoples and the spread of culture.

133. Under ordinary circumstances I do not satisfy myself that I have two hands by seeing how it looks. *Why* not? Has experience shown it to be unnecessary? Or (again): Have we in some way learnt a universal law of induction, and do we trust it here too?—But why should we have learnt one *universal* law first, and not the special one straight away?

134. After putting a book in a drawer, I assume it is there, unless. . . . "Experience always proves me right. There is no well attested case of a book's (simply) disappearing." It has *often* happened that a book has never turned up again, although we thought we knew for certain where it was.—But experience does really teach that a book, say, does not vanish away. (E.g. gradually evaporate.) But is it this experience with books etc. that leads us to assume that such a book has not vanished away? Well, suppose we were to find that under particular novel circumstances books did vanish away.—Shouldn't we alter our assumption? Can one give the lie to the effect of experience on our system of assumption?

135. But do we not simply follow the principle that what has always happened will happen again (or something like it)? What does it mean to follow this principle? Do we really introduce it into our reasoning? Or is it merely the *natural law* which our inferring apparently follows? This latter it may be. It is not an item in our considerations.

136. When Moore says he *knows* such and such, he is really enumerating a lot of empirical propositions which we affirm without special testing; propositions, that is, which have a peculiar logical role in the system of our empirical propositions.

137. Even if the most trustworthy of men assures me that he *knows* things are thus and so, this by itself cannot satisfy me that he does know. Only that he believes he knows. That is why Moore's assurance that he knows ... does not interest us. The propositions, however, which Moore retails as examples of such known truths are indeed interesting. Not because anyone knows their truth, or believes he knows them, but because they all have a *similar* role in the system of our empirical judgments.

138. We don't, for example, arrive at any of them as a result of investigation.

There are e.g. historical investigations and investigations into the shape and also the age of the earth, but not into whether the earth has existed during the last hundred years. Of course many of us have information about this period from our parents and grandparents; but mayn't they be wrong?—"Nonsense!" one will say. "How should all these people be wrong?"—But is that an argument? Is it not simply the rejection of an idea? And perhaps the determination of a concept? For if I speak of a possible mistake here, this changes the role of "mistake" and "truth" in our lives.

139. Not only rules, but also examples are needed for establishing a practice. Our rules leave loop-holes open, and the practice has to speak for itself.

140. We do not learn the practice of making empirical judgments by learning rules: we are taught *judgments* and their connexion with other judgments. *A totality* of judgments is made plausible to us.

141. When we first begin to *believe* anything, what we believe is not a single proposition, it is a whole system of propositions. (Light dawns gradually over the whole.)

142. It is not single axioms that strike me as obvious, it is a system in which consequences and premises give one another *mutual* support.

143. I am told, for example, that someone climbed this mountain many years ago. Do I always enquire into the reliability of the teller of this story, and whether the mountain did exist years ago? A child learns there are reliable and unreliable informants much later than it

learns facts which are told it. It doesn't learn *at all* that that mountain has existed for a long time: that is, the question whether it is so doesn't arise at all. It swallows this consequence down, so to speak, together with *what* it learns.

144. The child learns to believe a host of things. I.e. it learns to act according to these beliefs. Bit by bit there forms a system of what is believed, and in that system some things stand unshakeably fast and some are more or less liable to shift. What stands fast does so, not because it is intrinsically obvious or convincing; it is rather held fast by what lies around it.

145. One wants to say "*All* my experiences shew that it is so". But how do they do that? For that proposition to which they point itself belongs to a particular interpretation of them.

"That I regard this proposition as certainly true also characterizes my interpretation of experience."

146. We form *the picture* of the earth as a ball floating free in space and not altering essentially in a hundred years. I said "We form the *picture* etc." and this picture now helps us in the judgment of various situations.

I may indeed calculate the dimensions of a bridge, sometimes calculate that here things are more in favour of a bridge than a ferry, etc. etc.,—but somewhere I must begin with an assumption or a decision.

147. The picture of the earth as a ball is a *good* picture, it proves itself everywhere, it is also a simple picture—in short, we work with it without doubting it.

148. Why do I not satisfy myself that I have two feet when I want to get up from a chair? There is no why. I simply don't. This is how I act.

149. My judgments themselves characterize the way I judge, characterize the nature of judgment.

150. How does someone judge which is his right and which his left hand? How do I know that my judgment will agree with someone else's? How do I know that this colour is blue? If I don't trust *myself*

here, why should I trust anyone else's judgment? Is there a why? Must I not begin to trust somewhere? That is to say: somewhere I must begin with not-doubting; and that is not, so to speak, hasty but excusable: it is part of judging.

151. I should like to say: Moore does not *know* what he asserts he knows, but it stands fast for him, as also for me; regarding it as absolutely solid is part of our *method* of doubt and enquiry.

152. I do not explicitly learn the propositions that stand fast for me. I can *discover* them subsequently like the axis around which a body rotates. This axis is not fixed in the sense that anything holds it fast, but the movement around it determines its immobility.

153. No one ever taught me that my hands don't disappear when I am not paying attention to them. Nor can I be said to presuppose the truth of this proposition in my assertions etc., (as if they rested on it) while it only gets sense from the rest of our procedure of asserting.

154. There are cases such that, if someone gives signs of doubt where we do not doubt, we cannot confidently understand his signs as signs of doubt.
I.e.: if we are to understand his signs of doubt as such, he may give them only in particular cases and may not give them in others.

155. In certain circumstances a man cannot make a *mistake.* ("Can" is here used logically, and the proposition does not mean that a man cannot say anything false in those circumstances.) If Moore were to pronounce the opposite of those propositions which he declares certain, we should not just not share his opinion: we should regard him as demented.

156. In order to make a mistake, a man must already judge in conformity with mankind.

157. Suppose a man could not remember whether he had always had five fingers or two hands? Should we understand him? Could we be sure of understanding him?

158. Can I be making a mistake, for example, in thinking that the words of which this sentence is composed are English words whose meaning I know?

159. As children we learn facts; e.g., that every human being has a brain, and we take them on trust. I believe that there is an island, Australia, of such-and-such a shape, and so on and so on; I believe that I had great-grandparents, that the people who gave themselves out as my parents really were my parents, etc. This belief may never have been expressed; even the thought that it was so, never thought.

160. The child learns by believing the adult. Doubt comes *after* belief.

161. I learned an enormous amount and accepted it on human authority, and then I found some things confirmed or disconfirmed by my own experience.

162. In general I take as true what is found in text-books, of geography for example. Why? I say: All these facts have been confirmed a hundred times over. But how do I know that? What is my evidence for it? I have a world-picture. Is it true or false? Above all it is the substratum of all my enquiring and asserting. The propositions describing it are not all equally subject to testing.

163. Does anyone ever test whether this table remains in existence when no one is paying attention to it?
We check the story of Napoleon, but not whether all the reports about him are based on sense-deception, forgery and the like. For whenever we test anything, we are already presupposing something that is not tested. Now am I to say that the experiment which perhaps I make in order to test the truth of a proposition presupposes the truth of the proposition that the apparatus I believe I see is really there (and the like)?

164. Doesn't testing come to an end?

165. One child might say to another: "I know that the earth is already hundreds of years old" and that would mean: I have learnt it.

166. The difficulty is to realize the groundlessness of our believing.

11

Hans Reichenbach, "The Search for Certainty," from *The Rise of Scientific Philosophy*

Hans Reichenbach (1891–1953) was a very highly thought of German-American philosopher whose main field was the philosophy of science. He was closely associated with the Vienna Circle, a group of logical positivists which flourished in the 1920s and 1930s. He taught from 1938 until his death at the University of California.

What the preceding chapter has shown is that the obscure conceptions of philosophical systems originate in certain *extralogical motives* intervening in the process of thought. The legitimate search for explanation in terms of generality is offered a pseudosatisfaction through picture language. Such an intrusion of poetry into knowledge is abetted by an urge for the construction of an imaginary world of pictures, which can become stronger than the quest for truth. The urge for picture-thinking may be called an extralogical motive because it does not represent a form of logical analysis but originates from mental needs outside the realm of logic.

There is a second extralogical motive which often interferes with the process of analysis. While knowledge acquired by sense observation is on the whole successful in everyday life, it is early recognized as being none too reliable. There are a few simple physical laws that seem to hold without exception, like the law that fire is hot, or that humans are mortal, or that unsupported bodies fall downward; but there are too many other rules which do have exceptions, like the rule that a seed planted in the ground will grow, or the rules of the weather, or the rules for the cure of human diseases. And a more comprehensive observation often reveals exceptions even to the stricter laws. For

From Hans Reichenbach, *The Rise of Scientific Philosophy*, Berkeley, University of California Press, 1951.

instance, the fire of fireflies is not hot, at least not in the usual sense of the word "hot"; and soap bubbles may rise into the air. While these exceptions can be taken care of by a more precise wording of the law, stating the conditions of its validity and the meanings of its terms more carefully, there usually remains a doubt whether the new formulation is free from exception, whether we can be sure that later discoveries will not reveal some limitation of the improved formulation. The development of science, with its repeated elimination of older theories and their replacement by new ones, supplies good reasons for such doubt.

There is another source of doubt: it is the fact that our personal experiences divide into a world of reality and a world of dream. That such a division must be made is, historically speaking, a discovery of a rather late period of the evolution of man; we know that the primitive peoples of our day do not possess a clear delineation of the two worlds. A primitive man who dreams that another man attacks him may take his dream for reality and go and kill the other man; or when he dreams that his wife deceives him with another man he may proceed to similar acts of vengeance, or acts of justice, the terminology depending on the point of view. A psychoanalyst might be willing to excuse the man to some extent by pointing out that such dreams will not occur without grounds and may justify, if not the retribution, at least the suspicion. The primitive man, however, acts not on the basis of psychoanalytical considerations, but because he lacks a clear distinction between dream and reality. Although the common-sense man of our day usually feels comfortably immune against such confusion, a little analysis reveals that his confidence cannot claim certainty. For while we dream we do not know that we are dreaming; it is only later, after awaking, that we recognize our dream as a dream. How then can we claim that our present experiences are of a more reliable type than those of a dream? The fact that they are associated with a feeling of reality does not make them more dependable, because we have the same feeling in a dream. We cannot completely exclude the possibility that later experiences will prove that we are dreaming even now. The argument is not raised in order to dissuade the common-sense man from his trust in his experiences; it shows, however, that we cannot claim absolute reliability for such trust.

The philosopher has always been troubled by the unreliability of sense perception, which he has illustrated by considerations like the given ones; in addition, he has mentioned sense illusions in the waking state, such as the apparent bending of a stick partly immersed in water, or the mirage in the desert. He therefore rejoiced to find at least one domain of knowledge which appeared exempt from deceit: that was mathematical knowledge.

Plato, as mentioned above, regarded mathematics as the supreme form of all knowledge. His influence has greatly contributed to the widespread conception that unless knowledge is of a mathematical form it is not knowledge at all. The modern scientist, despite his use of mathematics as a powerful instrument of research, would not accept this maxim unconditionally. He would insist that observation cannot be omitted from empirical science and would leave to mathematics merely the function of establishing connections between the various results of empirical investigation. He is very willing to use these mathematical connections as a guide to new observational discoveries; but he knows that they can help him only because he starts with observational material, and he is always ready to abandon mathematical conclusions if they are not confirmed by later observation. Empirical science, in the modern sense of the phrase, is a successful combination of mathematical with observational method. Its results are regarded, not as absolutely certain, but as highly probable and sufficiently reliable for all practical purposes.

To Plato, however, the concept of empirical knowledge would have appeared an absurdity. When he identified knowledge with mathematical knowledge, he wanted to say that observation should play no part in knowledge. "Arguments from probabilities are impostors", so we learn from one of Socrates' disciples in the dialogue *Phaedo*. Plato wanted certainty, not the inductive reliability which modern physics regards as its only attainable goal.

It is true, of course, that the Greeks had no science of physics comparable to ours and that Plato did not know how much might be achieved through the combination of mathematical method with experience. Nevertheless, there was one natural science which even in Plato's day had had great success with such a combination, the science of astronomy. The mathematical laws of the revolution of the stars and planets had been uncovered, to a high degree of perfection, by skillful observation and geometrical reasoning. But Plato was not willing to admit the contribution of observation to astronomy. He insisted that astronomy was knowledge only inasmuch as the motions of the stars were "apprehended by reason and intelligence". According to him, observations of the stars could not tell us very much about the laws governing their revolution, because their actual motion is imperfect and not strictly controlled by laws. It would be absurd, says Plato, to assume that the real motions of the stars are "eternal and subject to no deviation". He makes it very clear what he thinks of the observational astronomer: "Whether a man gapes at the heavens or blinks on the ground, seeking to learn some particular of sense, I would deny that he can learn, for nothing of that sort is matter of science; his soul is looking downwards, not upwards, whether his way to knowledge is by water or by land, whether he floats, or only lies on his back". Instead of observing the stars, we should try to find the laws of their revolution through thinking. The astronomer should "let the heavens alone" and approach his subject matter by the use of "the natural gift of reason" (*Republic* VII, pp. 529–530). Empirical science could not be rejected more strongly than in these words, which express the conviction that knowledge of nature does not require observation and is attainable through reason alone.

How can this antiempirical attitude be explained psychologically? It is the search for certainty which makes the philosopher disregard the contribution of observation to knowledge. Since he wants absolutely certain knowledge, he cannot accept the results of observations; since arguments from probabilities are for him impostors, he turns to mathematics as the only admissible source of truth. The ideal of the complete mathematization of knowledge, of a physics which is of the same type as geometry and arithmetic, springs from the desire to find absolute certainty for the laws of nature. It leads to the absurd demand that the physicist forget about his observations, that the astronomer turn his eyes away from the stars.

The kind of philosophy which regards reason as a source of knowledge of the physical world has been called *rationalism*. This word and its adjective *rationalistic* must be carefully distinguished from the word *rational*. Scientific knowledge is attained by the use of rational methods, because it requires the use of reason in application to observational material. But it is not rationalistic. This predicate would apply not to scientific method, but to a philosophical method which regards reason as a source of synthetic knowledge about the world and does not require observation for the verification of such knowledge.

In philosophical literature, the name *rationalism* is often restricted to certain rationalistic systems of the modern era, from which the systems of the Platonic type are distinguished as *idealism*. In the present book the name *rationalism* will always be used in the wider sense, so as to include idealism. This notation appears justified because both kinds of philosophy are alike inasmuch as they regard reason as an independent source of knowledge of the physical world. The psychological root of all rationalism in the wider sense is an extralogical motive, that is, a motive not justifiable in terms of logic: it is the search for certainty.

Plato was not the first rationalist. His most important predecessor was the mathematician-philosopher Pythagoras (about 540 B.C.), whose doctrines greatly influenced Plato. It appears understandable that the mathematician is more likely than others to turn rationalist. Knowing the success of logical deduction in a subject matter that does not require a reference to observation, he may be inclined to believe that his methods can be extended to other subject matters. The result is a theory of knowledge in which acts of insight replace sense perception, and in which reason is believed to possess a power of its own by means of which it discovers the general laws of the physical world.

Once empirical observation is abandoned as a source of truth, it is then but a short step to mysticism. If reason can create knowledge, other creations of the human mind may appear as trustworthy as knowledge. From this conception results a strange blend of mysticism and mathematics, which has never died out since its origin in Pythagoras' philosophy. His religious veneration of number and logic led him to the statement that all things are numbers, a doctrine hardly translatable into meaningful terms. The theory of the migration of the soul, discussed above in the context of Plato's theory of ideas, was one of the chief doctrines of Pythagoras, who is assumed to have taken it over from oriental religions. We know that Plato was acquainted with this doctrine through his connection with Pythagoreans. The conception that logical insight can reveal properties of the physical world is also Pythagorean in origin. Pythagoras' followers practiced a sort of religious cult, the mystical character of which is visible in certain taboos said to have been imposed upon them by the master. For instance, they were taught that it is dangerous to leave an impress of the body on one's bed and were required to straighten out their bedclothes when they got up in the morning.

There are other forms of mysticism, which are not associated with mathematics. The mystic usually has an antirational and antilogical bias and shows contempt for the power of reason. He claims possession of some sort of supernatural experience, which presents him with infallible truth through a visionary act. This kind of mysticism is known from religious mystics. Outside the realm of religion, antirational mysticism has not played an important part, and I may omit its discussion in this book, which is concerned with the analysis of forms of philosophy that are related to scientific thought and have contributed to the great controversy between philosophy and science. Only a mathematically inclined mysticism falls into the scope of this analysis. What unites such a mathematical mysticism with nonmathematical forms is the reference to acts of supersensuous vision; what distinguishes it from those other forms is the use of vision for the establishment of intellectual truth.

Of course, rationalism is not invariably mystical. Logical analysis in itself may be employed for the establishment of a kind of knowledge which is regarded as absolutely certain and yet as connected with knowledge of everyday life or scientific knowledge. Modern times have produced various rationalist systems of this nonmystical scientific type.

Among such systems I should like to discuss the rationalism of the French philosopher Descartes (1596–1650). In various writings he presented arguments for the uncertainty of perceptual knowledge, arguments of the kind mentioned above. It seems that he was extremely troubled by the uncertainty of all knowledge; he promised the Holy Virgin a pilgrimage to Loretto if she would illuminate his mind and help him find absolute certainty. He reports that the illumination came to him while he was living in an oven during a winter campaign in which he participated as an officer; and he expressed his gratitude to the Holy Virgin by fulfilling his vow.

Descartes' proof for absolute certainty is constructed by means of a logical trick. I can doubt everything, he argues, except one thing: that is the fact that I doubt. But when I doubt I think; and when I think I must exist. He thus claims to have proved the existence of the ego by logical reasoning; I think, therefore, I am, so goes his magical formula. When I call this inference a logical trick, I do not wish to say that Descartes intended to deceive his readers; I would rather say that he was himself deceived by this tricky form of reasoning. But logically speaking, the step from doubt to certainty performed in Descartes' inference resembles a sleight of hand—from doubting he proceeds to considering doubt as an action of an *ego,* and thus believes that he has found some fact which cannot be doubted.

Later analysis has shown the fallacy in Descartes' argument. The concept of the ego is not of so simple a nature as Descartes believed. We do not see our own selves in the way we see houses and people around us. We may perhaps speak of an observation of our acts of

thought, or of doubt; they are not perceived, however, as the products
of an ego, but as separate objects, as images accompanied by feelings.
To say "I think" goes beyond the immediate experience in that the
sentence employs the word "I". The statement "I think" represents
not an observational datum, but the end of long chains of thought
which uncover the existence of an ego as distinct from the ego of other
persons. Descartes should have said "there is thought", thus indicating
the sort of detached occurrence of the contents of thought, their emer-
gence independent of acts of volition or other attitudes involving the
ego. But then Descartes' inference could no longer be made. If the
existence of the ego is not warranted by immediate awareness, its
existence cannot be asserted with higher certainty than that of other
objects derived by means of plausible additions to observational data.

It is scarcely necessary to go into a more detailed refutation of
Descartes' inference. Even if the inference were tenable it would not
prove very much and could not establish certainty of our knowledge
about things other than the ego—that much is clear through the way
Descartes continues the argument. He first infers that because there
is an ego there must be God; or else the ego could not have the idea
of an infinite being. He goes on to infer that then the things around
us must also exist, since otherwise God would be an impostor. That
is a theological argument, which appears strange enough when offered
by so eminent a mathematician as Descartes. The interesting question
is: how is it possible that a logical issue, the attainability of certainty,
was dealt with by a maze of arguments composed of tricks and theology,
arguments that cannot be taken seriously by any scientifically trained
reader of our day?

The psychology of philosophers is a problem which deserves more
attention than is usually paid to it in the presentations of the history
of philosophy. Its study is likely to throw more light on the meaning
of philosophical systems than all attempts at a logical analysis of these
systems. There is poor logic in Descartes' inference, but there is a
great deal of psychological information to be gathered from it. It was
the search for certainty which made this excellent mathematician drift
into such muddled logic. It seems that the search for certainty can
make a man blind to the postulates of logic, that the attempt to base
knowledge on reason alone can make him abandon the principles of
cogent reasoning.

Psychologists explain the search for certainty as the desire to return
to the early days of infancy, which were not troubled by doubt and

were guided by the confidence in parental wisdom. This desire is usually intensified by an education which conditions the child to regard doubt as sin and confidence as a religious command. The biographer of Descartes might attempt to combine this general explanation with the religious tinge of Descartes' doubts, his prayer for illumination and his pilgrimage, which indicate that this man needed his philosophical system in order to overcome a deeply rooted complex of uncertainty. Without entering into a specific study of Descartes' case, one may draw an important conclusion from it: if the result of a logical inquiry is determined by a preconceived aim, if logic is made the instrument of proof of a result which we wish to establish for some other reason, the logic of the argument is prone to be fallacious. Logic can thrive only in an atmosphere of perfect freedom, on a ground whose extracts do not burden it with remnants of fear and prejudice. He who inquires into the nature of knowledge should keep his eyes open and be willing to accept any result that cogent reasoning brings to light; it does not matter if the result contradicts his conception of what knowledge should be. The philosopher must not make himself the servant of his desires.

This maxim seems to be trivial, but only because we do not realize how difficult it is to follow the maxim. The search for certainty is one of the most dangerous sources of error because it is associated with the claim of a superior knowledge. The certainty of logical proof is thus regarded as the ideal of knowledge; and the requirement is introduced that all knowledge should be established by methods as reliable as logic. In order to see the consequences of this conception, let us study more closely the nature of logical proof.

Logical proof is called *deduction;* the conclusion is obtained by deducing it from other statements, called the premises of the argument. The argument is so constructed that if the premises are true the conclusion must also be true. For instance, from the two statements "all men are mortal" and "Socrates is a man", we can derive the conclusion "Socrates is mortal". The example illustrates the emptiness of deduction: the conclusion cannot state more than is said in the premises; it merely makes explicit some consequence which is contained implicitly in the premises. It unwraps, so to speak, the conclusion that was wrapped up in the premises.

The value of deduction is grounded in its emptiness. For the very reason that the deduction does not add anything to the premises, it may always be applied without a risk of leading to a failure. More precisely speaking, the conclusion is no less reliable than the premises.

It is the logical function of deduction to transfer truth from given statements to other statements—but that is all it can do. It cannot establish synthetic truth unless another synthetic truth is already known.

The premises of the example, "all men are mortal" and "Socrates is a man", are both empirical truths, that is, truths derived from observation. The conclusion "Socrates is mortal", consequently, is also an empirical truth, and has no more certainty than the premises. Philosophers have always attempted to find premises of a better kind, which would not be subject to any criticism. Descartes believed that he had an unquestionable truth in his premise "I doubt". It was explained above that the term "I" in this premise can be questioned and that the inference cannot supply absolute certainty. The rationalist, however, will not give up, but will continue to look for unquestionable premises.

Now there are premises of this kind; they are given by the principles of logic. For instance: that every entity is identical with itself, and that every sentence is either true or false—the "to be or not to be" of the logician—are unquestionable premises. The trouble with them is that they, too, are empty. They state nothing about the physical world. They are rules for our description of the physical world, but do not contribute to the content of the description; they determine only its form, that is, the language of our description. The principles of logic, therefore, are *analytic.* (The term was introduced above as meaning "self-explanatory and empty".) In contrast, statements which inform us about a fact, such as observations with our eyes, are *synthetic,* that is, they add something to our knowledge. All the synthetic statements which experience presents to us, however, are subject to doubt and cannot provide us with absolutely certain knowledge.

An attempt to establish the desired certainty on an analytic premise was made in the famous *ontological* proof of God's existence, constructed by Anselm of Canterbury in the eleventh century. The demonstration begins with the definition of God as an infinitely perfect being; since such a being must have all essential properties, it must also have the property of existence. Therefore, so goes the conclusion, God exists. The premise, in fact, is analytic, because every definition is. Since the statement of God's existence is synthetic, the inference represents a trick by which a synthetic conclusion is derived from an analytic premise.

The fallacious nature of this inference is easily seen from its absurd consequences. If it is permissible to derive existence from a definition, we could demonstrate the existence of a cat with three tails by defining such an animal as a cat which has three tails and which exists. Logically speaking, the fallacy consists in a confusion of universals with particulars. From the definition we can only infer the universal statement that if something is a cat with three tails it exists, which is a true statement. But the particular statement that there is a cat with three tails cannot be derived. Similarly, we can infer from Anselm's definition only the statement that if something is an infinitely perfect being it exists, but not that there is such a being. (Anselm's confusion of universals and particulars, incidentally, is cognate to a similar confusion existing in the Aristotelian theory of the syllogism.)

It was Immanuel Kant (1724–1804) who saw that certainty of a synthetic nature cannot be derived from analytic premises but requires synthetic premises of unquestionable truth. Believing that such statements exist, he called them *synthetic a priori*. The word "a priori" means "not derived from experience", or "derived from reason and necessarily true". Kant's philosophy represents the great attempt to prove that there are synthetic a-priori truths; and historically speaking it represents the last great construction of a rationalist philosophy. He is superior to his predecessors Plato and Descartes in his avoidance of their mistakes. He does not commit himself to an existence of Platonic ideas; nor does he smuggle in a pseudonecessary premise by a trick, as Descartes does. He claims to have found the synthetic a priori in the principles of mathematics and mathematical physics. Like Plato, he starts with mathematical knowledge; he explains such knowledge, however, not by the existence of objects of a higher reality, but by an ingenious interpretation of empirical knowledge, to be discussed presently.

If progress in the history of philosophy consists in the discovery of significant questions, Kant is to be assigned a high rank because of his question concerning the existence of a synthetic a priori. Like other philosophers, however, he claims merit not for the question but for his answer to it. He even formulates the question in a somewhat different way. He is so convinced of the existence of a synthetic a priori that he regards it as hardly necessary to ask whether there is one; therefore, he poses his question in the form: how is a synthetic a priori possible? The proof of its existence, he concludes, is supplied by mathematics and mathematical physics.

There is very much to be said in defense of Kant's position. That he regards the axioms of geometry as synthetic a priori bears witness to a deep insight into the peculiar problems of geometry. Kant saw

that Euclid's geometry occupied a unique position in that it revealed
necessary relations holding for empirical objects, relations which could
not be regarded as analytic. He is much more explicit than Plato about
this point. Kant knew that the strictness of mathematical proof cannot
account for the empirical truth of geometrical theorems. Geometrical
propositions, such as the theorem about the angular sum of a triangle,
or Pythagoras' theorem, are derivable by strict logical deduction from
the axioms. But these axioms themselves are not so derivable—they
cannot be derivable because every derivation of synthetic conclusions
has to start with synthetic premises. The truth of the axioms must
therefore be established by other means than logic; they must be
synthetic a priori. Once the axioms are known to be true for physical
objects, the applicability of the theorems to these objects is then guaran-
teed by logic, since the truth of the axioms is transferred by the logical
derivation to the theorems. Conversely, if one is convinced that geometrical theorems apply to physical reality, one admits belief in the truth
of the axioms and therefore in a synthetic a priori. Even those persons
who would not like to commit themselves openly to a synthetic a priori
indicate through their behavior that they believe in it: they do not
hesitate to apply the results of geometry to practical measurements.
This argument, Kant maintains, proves the existence of the synthetic
a priori.

Kant contends that similar arguments can be constructed from mathematical physics. Ask a physicist, he explains, what is the weight of
smoke; he will ascertain it by weighing the substance before the burning
and then deducting the weight of the ashes. In this determination of
the weight of the smoke the assumption is expressed that mass is
indestructible. The principle of the conservation of mass, Kant argues,
is thus shown to be a synthetic a-priori truth, which the physicist
recognizes through the method of his experiment. We know today that
the computation described by Kant leads to the wrong result, because
it does not take into account the weight of the oxygen which enters
into a chemical combination with the burning substance. Had Kant
known of this discovery of a later time, however, he would have argued
that, although it modifies the mode of computation, it does not contradict the principle of the conservation of mass; this principle will supply
once more the frame of the computation if the weight of the oxygen
is included in the consideration.

Another synthetic a priori of the physicist, according to Kant, is the
principle of causality. Although we often are unable to find the cause

of an observed event, we do not assume that it occurred without a cause; we are convinced that we shall find the cause if we only go on searching for it. This conviction determines the method of scientific research and is the propelling force of every scientific experiment; if we did not believe in causality, there would be no science. As in the other arguments constructed by Kant, the existence of the synthetic a priori is here proved by reference to scientific procedure: science presupposes the synthetic a priori—this contention is the basis of Kant's philosophical system.

What makes Kant's position so strong is its scientific background. His search for certainty is not of the mystical type that appeals to an insight into a world of ideas, nor of the type that resorts to logical tricks which extract certainty from empty presuppositions, as a magician pulls a rabbit out of an empty hat. Kant mobilizes the science of his day for the proof that certainty is attainable; and he claims that the philosopher's dream of certainty is borne out by the results of science. From the appeal to the authority of the scientist Kant derives his strength.

But the ground on which Kant built was not so firm as he believed it to be. He regarded the physics of Newton as the ultimate stage of knowledge of nature and idealized it into a philosophical system. In deriving from pure reason the principles of Newtonian physics, he believed he had achieved the complete rationalization of knowledge, had attained the goal which his predecessors had been unable to reach. The title of his major work, *Critique of Pure Reason,* indicates his program of making reason the source of a synthetic a-priori knowledge and thus to establish as a necessary truth, on a philosophical ground, the mathematics and physics of his day.

It is a strange matter of fact that those who watch and admire scientific research from the outside frequently have more confidence in its results than the men who coöperate in its progress. The scientist knows about the difficulties which he had to eliminate before he could establish his theories. He is aware of the good luck which helped him discover theories that fit the given observations and which made later observations fit his theories. He realizes that discrepancies and new difficulties may arise at any moment, and he will never claim to have found the ultimate truth. Like the disciple who is more fanatical than the prophet, the philosopher of science is in danger of investing more confidence in scientific results than is warranted by their origin in observation and generalization.

The overestimation of the reliability of scientific results is not restricted to the philosopher; it has become a general feature of modern times, that is, of the period dating from the time of Galileo to our day, in which period falls the creation of modern science. The belief that science has the answer to all questions—that if somebody is in need of technical information, or is ill, or is troubled by some psychological problem, he merely has to ask the scientist in order to obtain an answer—is so widespread that science has taken over a social function which originally was satisfied by religion: the function of offering ultimate security. The belief in science has replaced, in large measure, the belief in God. Even where religion was regarded as compatible with science, it was modified by the mentality of the believer in scientific truth. The period of Enlightenment, into which Kant's lifework falls, did not abandon religion; but it transformed religion into a creed of reason, it made God a mathematical scientist who knew everything because he had a perfect insight into the laws of reason. No wonder the mathematical scientist appeared as a sort of little god, whose teachings had to be accepted as exempt from doubt. All the dangers of theology, its dogmatism and its control of thought through the guaranty of certainty, reappear in a philosophy that regards science as infallible.

Had Kant lived to see the physics and mathematics of our day he might very well have abandoned the philosophy of the synthetic a priori. So let us regard his books as documents of their time, as the attempt to appease his hunger for certainty by his belief in the physics of Newton. In fact, Kant's philosophical system must be conceived as an ideological superstructure erected on the foundation of a physics modeled for an absolute space, an absolute time, and an absolute determinism of nature. This origin explains the system's success and its failure, explains why Kant has been regarded by so many as the greatest philosopher of all time, and why his philosophy has nothing to say to us who are witnesses of the physics of Einstein and Bohr.

This origin also accounts for the psychological fact that Kant did not see the weak spot in the logical construction by which he intended to justify the synthetic a priori. It is the preconceived aim that makes the philosopher blind to the tacit assumptions he has introduced. In order to make my criticism clear, I will now discuss the second part of Kant's theory of the synthetic a priori, in which he proceeds to answer the question "how is the synthetic a priori possible?"

Kant claimed he could explain the occurrence of a synthetic a priori through a theory which shows the a-priori principles to be necessary conditions of experience. He argues that mere observation does not supply experience, that observations must be ordered and organized before they can become knowledge. The organization of knowledge, according to him, is dependent on the use of certain principles, such as the axioms of geometry and the principles of causality and the conservation of mass, which are innate in the human mind and which we employ as regulative principles in the construction of science. They are, so he concludes, necessarily valid because without them science would be impossible. He calls this proof the transcendental deduction of the synthetic a priori.

It must be recognized that Kant's interpretation of the synthetic a priori is widely superior to Plato's analysis of this point. In order to explain how reason can have knowledge of nature, Plato assumes that there exists a world of ideal things which reason perceives and which somehow controls the real objects. No such mysticism is found in Kant. Reason has knowledge of the physical world because it shapes the picture we construct of the physical world; that is Kant's argument. The synthetic a priori is of a subjective origin; it is a condition superimposed on human knowledge by the human mind.

Let me clarify Kant's explanation by a simple illustration. A man who wears blue spectacles will observe that everything is blue. If he were born with those glasses, however, he would regard blueness as a necessary predicate of all things, and it would take some time until he would discover that it is he, or rather his glasses, that introduce blueness into the world. The synthetic a-priori principles of physics and mathematics are the blue glasses through which we see the world. We should not be astonished that every experience will confirm them because we cannot acquire experience without them.*

This illustration does not stem from Kant; in fact, it appears alien

---

* The objection might be raised that a man born with blue glasses would not know other colors than blue and would therefore not conceive blue as a color. In order to avoid this consequence, let us assume that the man is born with his natural eye lenses colored blue, while his retina and his nervous system are normal. So far as his optical sensations were produced by internal stimulation, they would then be normal. The man would therefore be able to see other colors than blue in his dreams and come to the conclusion that the physical world is subject to restrictions which do not apply to the world of his imagination. He might very well eventually find out that this restriction stems from the composition of his eye lenses.

to the author of prolix books filled with abstract considerations in an involved language, which makes the reader thirst for concrete illustrations. Had Kant been accustomed to explain his ideas in the plain and simple language of the scientist he would perhaps have discovered that his transcendental deduction is of questionable value. He would have seen that his argument, if further extended, leads to an analysis of the following kind.

Assume it is correct that no experience can ever disprove the a-priori principles. This means that whatever observations will be made, it will always be possible to interpret or order them in such a way that these principles are satisfied. For instance, if measurements on triangles were made which contradicted the theorem of the angular sum, we would assign the deviations to observational errors and introduce "corrections" for the measured values in such a way that the geometrical theorem would be satisfied. But if the philosopher could prove that such a procedure is always possible for all a-priori principles, these principles would be shown to be empty and thus analytic; they would not restrict possible experiences and thus not inform us about properties of the physical world. An extension of Kant's theory in this direction was, in fact, attempted by H. Poincaré under the name of *conventionalism*. He regards the geometry of Euclid as a convention, that is, as an arbitrary rule which we impose upon our system of ordering experiences. To illustrate the meaning of conventionalism in a field other than geometry, consider the statement that all numbers larger than 99 must be written with at least three digits. This statement is true only for the decimal system, but would break down for another notation, such as the duodecimal system of the Babylonians, who used the number 12 as the basis of their number system. The decimal system is a convention which we use for our number notation, and we can prove that all numbers can be written in this notation. The statement that all numbers larger than 99 must be written with at least three digits is analytic when it refers to this system. In order to interpret Kant's philosophy as conventionalism, we would have to prove that Kant's principles can be carried through in the face of all possible experiences.

But such a proof cannot be given. In fact, if the a-priori principles are synthetic, as Kant believed, such a proof is impossible. The word "synthetic" means that we can imagine experiences which contradict the a-priori principles; and if we can imagine such experiences, we cannot exclude the possibility that some day we might have them. Kant would argue that this case cannot happen because the principles are necessary conditions of experience, or, in other words, because, in the case considered, experience as an ordered system of observations would not be possible. But how does he know that experience will always be possible? Kant had no proof that we would never arrive at a totality of observations which could not be ordered in the frame of his a-priori principles and which would make experience impossible, at least experience in the Kantian sense. In the language of our illustration this case would occur if the physical world contained no light rays of the wave length corresponding to blue; the man with the blue glasses would then see nothing. If the corresponding case were to occur in science, if experience of the Kantian kind should become impossible, Kant's principles would be shown to be invalid for the physical world. And because of the possibility of such a disproof, the principles cannot be called a priori. The postulate that experience in the frame of the a-priori principles must always be possible is the unwarranted assumption of Kant's system, is the undemonstrable premise on which his system hinges. That he does not explicitly state his premise shows that the search for certainty made him overlook the limitations of his argument.

I do not wish to be irreverent to the philosopher of the Enlightenment. We are able to raise this criticism because we have seen physics enter a stage in which the Kantian frame of knowledge does break down. The axioms of Euclidean geometry, the principles of causality and substance are no longer recognized by the physics of our day. We know that mathematics is analytic and that all applications of mathematics to physical reality, including physical geometry, are of an empirical validity and subject to correction by further experience; in other words, that there is no synthetic a priori. But it is only now, after the physics of Newton and the geometry of Euclid have been superseded, that such knowledge is ours. It is difficult to conceive of the possibility of a breakdown of a scientific system in its heyday; it is easy to refer to such a breakdown after it has become reality.

Such experience has made us wise enough to anticipate the breaking down of any system. It has not discouraged us, though. The new physics has shown that we can have knowledge outside the frame of the Kantian principles, that the human mind is not a rigid system of categories into which it packs all experiences, but that the principles of knowledge change with its content and can be adapted to a much more complicated world than that of Newtonian mechanics. We hope that in any future situation our minds will be flexible enough to supply methods of logical organization that can cope with the given observational material. That is a hope, not a belief for which we pretend to have a philosophical proof. We can do without certainty. But it was a long way to this more liberal attitude toward knowledge. The search for certainty had to burn itself out in the philosophical systems of the past before we were able to envisage a conception of knowledge which does away with all claims to eternal truth.

12

Norman Malcolm,
"Do I Know I Am Awake?"
from *Dreaming*

Norman Malcolm (1911–1989) taught philosophy at Cornell. He was a pupil of Wittgenstein's, of whom he wrote a celebrated memoir, Ludwig Wittgenstein: A Memoir, Oxford, 1958. *His work was concentrated on the theory of knowledge and perception, the philosophy of mind, and also the philosophy of religion.*

'There are recognized ways of distinguishing between dreaming and waking (how otherwise should we know how to use and to contrast the words?) . . .' (Austin, p. 133). I think Austin says this, not because he knows of any 'recognized ways', but because he assumes he can *know* he is awake and so must have some way of doing it. His question, 'How otherwise should we know how to use and to contrast the words?', assumes we do know how. This is partly right and partly wrong: we know how to use the words 'I am awake' but not the words 'I am dreaming'. To speak more exactly, we know that 'I am dreaming' is the first person singular present indicative of the verb 'dream', and that dreaming and waking are logical contraries, and therefore that 'I am dreaming' and 'I am awake' are logical contraries. In this sense we know how to use the sentence 'I am dreaming'. On the other hand, considerations previously mentioned bring home to us that it can never be a *correct* use of language to say (even to oneself) 'I am dreaming'. In this sense we do not know how to use those words. Yet we know that it is sometimes correct to say 'I am awake', and our inclination is to suppose that there must be some way, therefore, of telling that oneself is awake. In discussing the impossibility (or so he thought) of proving that he was holding his two hands up before him, as

From Norman Malcolm, *Dreaming*, London, Routledge, 1959.

he stood in front of his audience at the British Academy, Moore
says:

> In order to do it, I should need to prove for one thing, as Descartes
> pointed out, that I am not now dreaming. But how can I prove that I
> am not? I have, no doubt, conclusive reasons for asserting that I am
> not now dreaming; I have conclusive evidence that I am awake: but that
> is a very different thing from being able to prove it. I could not tell
> you what all my evidence is; and I should require to do this at least,
> in order to give you a proof.

Moore is greatly perplexed because, try as he might, he cannot bring
to mind all (or even *any*, as I think) of his evidence that he is awake;
and yet he is convinced that he has conclusive evidence, convinced
that he *knows* he is awake.

It is possible for a philosopher to think he knows some proposition,
p, to be true, because he realizes it would be absurd to affirm that *p*
is false or even *possibly* false—although he is quite unclear about the
nature of the absurdity. It may have been so with Moore. He realized
that it would have been a monstrous absurdity for him to declare that
he was not awake or that possibly he was not, and this may have
persuaded him that he *knew* he was awake. Having looked into the
reasons for the absurdity we see that this conclusion does not follow.
For our investigation proves (if we take 'not awake' as equivalent to
'asleep') that nothing counts for or *against* the truth of 'I am not awake',
and so nothing counts *for* the truth of 'I am awake'. If one cannot
observe or have evidence that one is *not* awake, one cannot observe or
have evidence that one *is* awake. No wonder Moore could not lay his
hands on a piece of evidence!

I think a person might have some sort of test for determining whether
he is *fully* awake. Suppose his job was to operate a machine and that
this was a dangerous thing to do when he was not fully awake. Having
just got up from a night's sleep he tries some simple feat of skill, like
balancing a coffee cup on the back of his hand, and if he cannot do
it he says 'I'm not completely awake yet; I'd better wait a bit before
starting that engine'. (Or he might have said 'I'm not awake yet': but
this would mean 'I'm half asleep' or 'I'm not completely awake'. Or
he might even have said 'I'm still asleep', but anyone would understand
him to have meant 'I'm not fully awake'.) Such a test may seem queer,

but I see no logical absurdity in it. What makes no sense is that he should apply to himself a test by which he might find out that he is *asleep*, not just half-asleep or not completely awake.

It was remarked previously (Chapter 5) that the actual use of the sentences 'Am I dreaming?' and 'I must be dreaming' is to express surprise at some appearance, and perhaps to question whether things are as they seem or to suggest that they are not. I think those sentences do not differ in their actual use in everyday life from the use of the sentences 'Do my senses deceive me?' and 'It must be that they do'. There are many ways of finding out whether one is presented with a false appearance: getting closer, waiting a bit and looking again, asking someone whether he sees what you do, and so on. It may be that part at least of the peculiar force of the philosophical question 'How can I tell whether I am dreaming now?' comes from our mixing up the actual use of the question 'Am I dreaming?' with what, in our philosophical thinking, we imagine *ought* to be its use. As a result we confuse the sometimes sensible question 'How can I tell whether that thing over there is actually the way it looks to be?' with the always senseless question 'How can I tell whether I am awake?' There are ways of telling that one is experiencing an hallucination or some sensory illusion, but no ways of telling that one is awake. Philosophers have commonly treated the questions 'Am I hallucinated?' and 'Am I asleep in a dream?' as if they are nearly equivalent, whereas in fact the former has sense in some circumstances and the latter never has sense.

Since I hold that it makes no sense to suppose that a man should doubt or question anything while he is asleep, it might be thought that my intention is to provide a demonstrative argument by which anyone who is perplexed by the question 'Am I awake or dreaming?' can determine that he is awake. For can he not argue as follows?: 'I am perplexed as to whether I am awake or dreaming in sleep. But it makes no sense to suppose that I should be perplexed while asleep. Therefore I am awake'. This form of reasoning would not, however, remove the perplexity of a determined philosophical sceptic, since he might say to himself: 'I admit that *if* I am perplexed I am awake; but am I perplexed or do I merely dream that I am?'. If the objection occurred to him: 'Since I am in doubt whether I am really perplexed or merely dream that I am, I must be awake', he might make to himself this rejoinder: 'I don't know whether I am actually in doubt or just dream that I doubt'. And so on *ad infinitum*. Nothing can force him to affirm that he *is* perplexed or in doubt and therefore nothing can force him to find in the above reasoning a demonstration that he is awake and not dreaming.[1]

It is not my aim, however, to propose a piece of reasoning by which someone can arrive at the knowledge that he is awake. My contribution (if it is one) to this renowned sceptical problem has been to try to show that the sentence 'I am not awake' is strictly senseless and does not express a possibility that one can think. This is to say that when the sentence 'I am awake' is used to make a statement, there is not another possible statement which is its proper negation. There are not two things for me to decide between, one that I am awake, the other that I am not awake. There is nothing to decide, no choice to make, nothing to find out. I cannot pass from not knowing whether I am awake or dreaming to knowing I am awake. To say 'I don't know whether I am awake or dreaming' would be to imply that 'I am dreaming' makes sense and expresses a possibility. Therefore the sentence 'I don't know whether I am awake or dreaming' cannot be a proper description of my condition, being itself a piece of nonsense. There cannot be such a thing as my lacking knowledge of whether I am awake or dreaming and so there cannot be a *transition* from that supposed privation to the knowledge that I am awake. There can be a transition from the belief that the sentence 'I am dreaming' makes sense to the knowledge that it does not, and this I have tried to provide. If someone wants to say that coming to know that the sentence 'I am dreaming' is nonsense is coming to know that one is awake, he is welcome to it, although this cannot fail to be a most misleading thing to say. Certainly you cannot be said to know *by observation* that you are awake: and since the fact that you are awake, when you are, is contingent, it would seem that if you knew it at all it would have to be by observation. You cannot know by observation that you are awake because if you could it would make sense to speak of knowing by observation that you are not awake. It is even more inappropriate to speak of knowing that one is awake than of knowing that one is in pain, for 'I am in pain' has a sensible negation at least. It appears to me that 'I know I am awake' either is redundant, meaning no more than 'I am awake', or else it means, 'The sentence "I am not awake" makes no sense'.

1. I am indebted to Mr. Geoffrey Warnock for this observation. Apparently some readers of my article 'Dreaming and Skepticism' thought my intention was to provide a method of proving to oneself that one is awake. It must be admitted that the article is not entirely clear on this point.

The temptation to hold that one knows by observation that one is awake is very powerful. One is inclined to think of the matter in something like this way: 'If someone, wanting to know whether I am asleep or awake, whispers to me "Are you awake?", I can reply "Yes, I'm awake". In making that reply I apply the word "awake" correctly to my state at the time. How can that be unless I *take note* of that state?' I think the imagery one has here is fairly clear. There are various states of oneself, each having a name. 'Awake' is the name of one of them, 'fear' of another, 'drowsy' of another, and so on. When I apply 'awake' to myself I *pick out* one state from others having different names. In order to pick it out I must take note of it, I must *see* it.

I think we go wrong in supposing that when I answer 'I'm awake', *I apply the word 'awake' correctly to my state at the time*—although that sounds unexceptionable. For what would it mean to apply that word *incorrectly* to my state at the time? When we say 'I'm awake' we are not *distinguishing* between states. It is not a matter of 'picking out' anything. When you say 'I'm awake' you are not reporting or describing your condition. You are *showing* someone that you are awake. There are countless other ways of doing this (one way would be to exclaim 'I'm not awake'); but the conventionally correct way of doing it with words is to say 'I am awake'.

The anciently perplexing question 'How can I tell whether I am awake or dreaming?' seems to me to obtain its force from two errors. One is that of supposing that dreaming and waking might be 'exact counterparts', this being an error that comes from confusing the historical and dream-telling senses of first person singular psychological sentences in the past tense. The other is that of thinking that one *must* be able to know, to *see*, that one is awake. We are thus brought to a state of paralysis, caught as it were in the grip of contradiction. We think we must *know* this, yet we realize that we could not. I have tried to expose both errors.

13

O. K. Bouwsma,
"Descartes' Evil Genius,"
from *Philosophical Essays*

O. K. Bouwsma (1898–1978) was a friend and follower of Wittgenstein. He wrote in the introduction to his Philosophical Essays, *in which "Descartes' Evil Genius" appeared, that "I have long hesitated to assume the risk of the incalculable harm these essays might do; but now, in view of the likewise incalculable good they might do, I have tossed a coin, and it came down just as I thought it would. It stood on its edge. And I knocked it down." The "Memorial Minutes" obituary of the American Philosophical Association for 1978 says of Bouwsma that "He taught many things, but he always aimed at one thing: Fear God and keep His commandments."*

There was once an evil genius who promised the mother of us all that if she ate of the fruit of the tree, she would be like God, knowing good and evil. He promised knowledge. She did eat and she learned, but she was disappointed, for to know good and evil and not to be God is awful. Many an Eve later, there was rumor of another evil genius. This evil genius promised no good, promised no knowledge. He made a boast, a boast so wild and so deep and so dark that those who heard it cringed in hearing it. And what was that boast? Well, that apart from a few, four or five, clear and distinct ideas, he could deceive any son of Adam about anything. So he boasted. And with some result? Some indeed! Men going about in the brightest noonday would look and exclaim: "How obscure!" and if some careless merchant counting his apples was heard to say: "Two and three are five," a hearer of the boast would rub his eyes and run away. This evil genius still whispers, thundering, among the leaves of books, frightening people, whispering: "I can. Maybe I will. Maybe so, maybe not." The tantalizer! In what follows I should like to examine the boast of this evil genius.

From O. K. Bouwsma, *Philosophical Essays*, Lincoln, University of Nebraska Press, 1965.

I am referring, of course, to that evil genius of whom Descartes writes:

> I shall then suppose, not that God who is supremely good and the fountain of truth, but some evil genius not less powerful than deceitful, has employed his whole energies in deceiving me. I shall consider that the heavens, the earth, the colors, figures, sound, and all other external things are nought but illusions and dreams of which this evil genius has availed himself, in order to lay traps for my credulity; I shall consider myself as having no hands, no eyes, no flesh, no blood, nor any senses, yet falsely believing myself to possess all these things.[1]

This then is the evil genius whom I have represented as boasting that he can deceive us about all these things. I intend now to examine this boast, and to understand how this deceiving and being deceived are to take place. I expect to discover that the evil genius may very well deceive us, but that if we are wary, we need not be deceived. He will deceive us, if he does, by bathing the word "illusion" in a fog. This then will be the word to keep our minds on. In order to accomplish all this, I intend to describe the evil genius carrying out his boast in two adventures. The first of these I shall consider a thoroughly transparent case of deception. The word "illusion" will find a clear and familiar application. Nevertheless in this instance the evil genius will not have exhausted "his whole energies in deceiving us." Hence we must aim to imagine a further trial of the boast, in which the "whole energies" of the evil genius are exhausted. In this instance I intend to show that the evil genius is himself befuddled, and that if we too exhaust some of our energies in sleuthing after the peculiarities in his diction, then we need not be deceived either.

Let us imagine the evil genius then at his ease meditating that very bad is good enough for him, and that he would let bad enough alone. All the old pseudos, pseudo names and pseudo statements, are doing very well. But today it was different. He took no delight in common lies, everyday fibs, little ones, old ones. He wanted something new and something big. He scratched his genius; he uncovered an idea. And he scribbled on the inside of his tattered halo, "Tomorrow, I will deceive," and he smiled, and his words were thin and like fine wire.

---

1. *Philosophical Works of Descartes,* trans. E. S. Haldane and G. R. T. Ross (2 vols.; Cambridge: Cambridge University Press, 1912), I, 147.

"Tomorrow I will change everything, everything, everything. I will change flowers, human beings, trees, hills, sky, the sun, and everything else into paper. Paper alone I will not change. There will be paper flowers, paper human beings, paper trees. And human beings will be deceived. They will think that there are flowers, human beings, and trees, and there will be nothing but paper. It will be gigantic. And it ought to work. After all men have been deceived with much less trouble. There was a sailor, a Baptist I believe, who said that all was water. And there was no more water then than there is now. And there was a pool-hall keeper who said that all was billiard balls. That's a long time ago of course, a long time before they opened one, and listening, heard that it was full of the sound of a trumpet. My prospects are good. I'll try it."

And the evil genius followed his own directions and did according to his words. And this is what happened.

Imagine a young man, Tom, bright today as he was yesterday, approaching a table where yesterday he had seen a bowl of flowers. Today it suddenly strikes him that they are not flowers. He stares at them troubled, looks away, and looks again. Are they flowers? He shakes his head. He chuckles to himself. "Huh! that's funny. Is this a trick? Yesterday there certainly were flowers in that bowl." He sniffs suspiciously, hopefully, but smells nothing. His nose gives no assurance. He thinks of the birds that flew down to peck at the grapes in the picture and of the mare that whinnied at the likeness of Alexander's horse. Illusions! The picture oozed no juice, and the likeness was still. He walked slowly to the bowl of flowers. He looked, and he sniffed, and he raised his hand. He stroked a petal lightly, lover of flowers, and he drew back. He could scarcely believe his fingers. They were not flowers. They were paper.

As he stands, perplexed, Milly, friend and dear, enters the room. Seeing him occupied with the flowers, she is about to take up the bowl and offer them to him, when once again he is overcome with feelings of strangeness. She looks just like a great big doll. He looks more closely, closely as he dares, seeing this may be Milly after all. Milly, are you Milly?—that wouldn't do. Her mouth clicks as she opens it, speaking, and it shuts precisely. Her forehead shines, and he shudders at the thought of Mme Tussaud's. Her hair is plaited, evenly, perfectly, like Milly's but as she raises one hand to guard its order, touching it, preening, it whispers like a newspaper. Her teeth are white as a genteel monthly. Her gums are pink, and there is a clapper in her mouth. He thinks of mama dolls, and of the rubber doll he used to pinch; it had a misplaced navel right in the pit of the back, that whistled. Galatea in paper! Illusions!

He noted all these details, flash by flash by flash. He reaches for a chair to steady himself and just in time. She approaches with the bowl of flowers, and, as the bowl is extended towards him, her arms jerk. The suppleness, the smoothness, the roundness of life is gone. Twitches of a smile mislight up her face. He extends his hand to take up the bowl and his own arms jerk as hers did before. He takes the bowl, and as he does so sees his hand. It is pale, fresh, snowy. Trembling, he drops the bowl, but it does not break, and the water does not run. What a mockery!

He rushes to the window, hoping to see the real world. The scene is like a theatre-set. Even the pane in the window is drawn very thin, like cellophane. In the distance are the forms of men walking about and tossing trees and houses and boulders and hills upon the thin cross section of a truck that echoes only echoes of chugs as it moves. He looks into the sky upward, and it is low. There is a patch straight above him, and one seam is loose. The sun shines out of the blue like a drop of German silver. He reaches out with his pale hand, crackling the cellophane, and his hand touches the sky. The sky shakes and tiny bits of it fall, flaking his white hand with confetti.

Make-believe!

He retreats, crinkling, creaking, hiding his sight. As he moves he misquotes a line of poetry: "Those are perils that were his eyes," and he mutters, "Hypocritical pulp!" He goes on: "I see that the heavens, the earth, colors, figures, sound, and all other external things, flowers, Milly, trees and rocks and hills are paper, paper laid as traps for my credulity. Paper flowers, paper Milly, paper sky!" Then he paused, and in sudden fright he asked "And what about me?" He reaches to his lip and with two fingers tears the skin and peels off a strip of newsprint. He looks at it closely, grim. "I shall consider myself as having no hands, no eyes, no flesh, no blood, or any senses." He lids his paper eyes and stands dejected. Suddenly he is cheered. He exclaims: "*Cogito me papyrum esse, ergo sum.*" He has triumphed over paperdom.

I have indulged in this phantasy in order to illustrate the sort of situation which Descartes' words might be expected to describe. The evil genius attempts to deceive. He tries to mislead Tom into thinking what is not. Tom is to think that these are flowers, that this is the Milly that was, that those are trees, hills, the heavens, etc. And he does this by creating illusions, that is, by making something that looks like flowers, artificial flowers; by making something that looks like and sounds like and moves like Milly, an artificial Milly. An illusion is something that looks like or sounds like, so much like, something else that you either mistake it for something else, or you can easily understand how someone might come to do this. So when the evil genius creates illusions intending to deceive he makes things which might quite easily be mistaken for what they are not. Now in the phantasy as I discovered it Tom is not deceived. He does experience the illusion, however. The intention of this is not to cast any reflection upon the deceptive powers of the evil genius. With such refinements in the paper art as we now know, the evil genius might very well have been less unsuccessful. And that in spite of his rumored lament: "And I made her of the best paper!" No, that Tom is not deceived, that he detects the illusion, is introduced in order to remind ourselves how illusions are detected. That the paper flowers are illusory is revealed by the recognition that they are paper. As soon as Tom realizes that though they look like flowers but are paper, he is acquainted with, sees through the illusion, and is not deceived. What is required, of course, is that he know the difference between flowers and paper, and that when presented with one or the other he can tell the difference. The attempt of the evil genius also presupposes this. What he intends is that though Tom knows this difference, the paper will look so much like flowers that Tom will not notice the respect in which the paper is different from the flowers. And even though Tom had actually been deceived and had not recognized the illusion, the evil genius himself must have been aware of the difference, for this is involved in his design. This is crucial, as we shall see when we come to consider the second adventure of the evil genius.

As you will remember I have represented the foregoing as an illustration of the sort of situation which Descartes' words might be expected to describe. Now, however, I think that this is misleading. For though I have described a situation in which there are many things, nearly all of which are calculated to serve as illusions, this question may still arise. Would this paper world still be properly described as a world of illusions? If Tom says: "These are flowers," or "These look like flowers" (uncertainly), then the illusion is operative. But if Tom says: "These are paper," then the illusion has been destroyed. Descartes uses the words: "And all other external things are nought but illusions."

This means that the situation which Descartes has in mind is such that if Tom says: "These are flowers," he will be wrong, but he will be wrong also if he says: "These are paper," and it won't matter what sentence of that type he uses. If he says: "These are rock"—or cotton or cloud or wood—he is wrong by the plan. He will be right only if he says: "These are illusions." But the project is to keep him from recognizing the illusions. This means that the illusions are to be brought about not by anything so crude as paper or even cloud. They must be made of the stuff that dreams are made of.

Now let us consider this second adventure.

The design then is this. The evil genius is to create a world of illusions. There are to be no flowers, no Milly, no paper. There is to be nothing at all, but Tom is every moment to go on mistaking nothing for something, nothing at all for flowers, nothing at all for Milly, etc. This is, of course, quite different from mistaking paper for flowers, paper for Milly. And yet all is to be arranged in such a way that Tom will go on just as we now do, and just as Tom did before the paper age, to see, hear, smell the world. He will love the flowers, he will kiss Milly, he will blink at the sun. So he thinks. And in thinking about these things he will talk and argue just as we do. But all the time he will be mistaken. There are no flowers, there is no kiss, there is no sun. Illusions all. This then is the end at which the evil genius aims.

How now is the evil genius to attain this end? Well, it is clear that a part of what he aims at will be realized if he destroys everything. Then there will be no flowers, and if Tom thinks that there are flowers he will be wrong. There will be no face that is Milly's and no tumbled beauty on her head, and if Tom thinks that there is Milly's face and Milly's hair, he will be wrong. It is necessary then to see to it that there are none of these things. So the evil genius, having failed with paper, destroys even all paper. Now there is nothing to see, nothing to hear, nothing to smell, etc. But this is not enough to deceive. For though Tom sees nothing, and neither hears nor smells anything, he may also think that he sees nothing. He must also be misled into thinking that he does see something, that there are flowers and Milly, and hands, eyes, flesh, blood, and all other senses. Accordingly the evil genius restores to Tom his old life. Even the memory of that paper day is blotted out, not a scrap remains. Witless Tom lives on, thinking, hoping, loving as he used to, unwitted by the great destroyer. All that seems so solid, so touchable to seeming hands, so biteable to apparent teeth, is so flimsy that were the evil genius to poke his index at it, it would curl away save for one tiny trace, the smirch of that index. So once more the evil genius has done according to his word.

And now let us examine the result.

I should like first of all to describe a passage of Tom's life. Tom is all alone, but he doesn't know it. What an opportunity for methodologico-metaphysico-solipsimo! I intend, in any case, to disregard the niceties of his being so alone and to borrow his own words, with the warning that the evil genius smiles as he reads them. Tom writes:

> Today, as usual, I came into the room and there was the bowl of flowers on the table. I went up to them, caressed them, and smelled over them. I thank God for flowers! There's nothing so real to me as flowers. Here the genuine essence of the world's substance, as its gayest and most hilarious speaks to me. It seems unworthy even to think of them as erect, and waving on pillars of sap. Sap! Sap!

There was more in the same vein, which we need not bother to record. I might say that the evil genius was a bit amused, snickered in fact, as he read the words "so real," "essence," "substance," etc., but later he frowned and seemed puzzled. Tom went on to describe how Milly came into the room, and how glad he was to see her. They talked about the flowers. Later he walked to the window and watched the gardener clearing a space a short distance away. The sun was shining, but there were a few heavy clouds. He raised the window, extended his hand and four large drops of rain wetted his hand. He returned to the room and quoted to Milly a song from *The Tempest*. He got all the words right, and was well pleased with himself. There was more he wrote, but this was enough to show how quite normal everything seems. And, too, how successful the evil genius is.

And the evil genius said to himself, not quite in solipsimo, "Not so, not so, not at all so."

The evil genius was, however, all too human. Admiring himself but unadmired, he yearned for admiration. To deceive but to be unsuspected is too little glory. The evil genius set about then to plant the seeds of suspicion. But how to do this? Clearly there was no suggestive paper to tempt Tom's confidence. There was nothing but Tom's mind, a stream of seemings and of words to make the seemings seem no seemings. The evil genius must have words with Tom and must engage the same seemings with him. To have words with Tom is to have the words together, to use them in the same way, and to engage the same seemings is to see and to hear and to point to the same. And so the evil genius, free spirit, entered in at the door of Tom's pineal gland and lodged there. He floated in the humors that flow, glandwise and sensewise, everywhere being as much one with Tom as difference will allow. He looked out of the same eyes, and when Tom pointed with his finger, the evil genius said "This" and meant what Tom, hearing, also meant, seeing. Each heard with the same ear what the other heard. For every sniffing of the one nose there were two identical smells, and there were two tactualities for every touch. If Tom had had a toothache, together they would have pulled the same face. The twinsomeness of two monads finds here the limit of identity. Nevertheless there was otherness looking out of those eyes as we shall see.

It seems then that on the next day, the evil genius "going to and fro" in Tom's mind and "walking up and down in it," Tom once again, as his custom was, entered the room where the flowers stood on the table. He stopped, looked admiringly, and in a caressing voice said: "Flowers! Flowers!" And he lingered. The evil genius, more subtle "than all the beasts of the field," whispered "Flowers? Flowers?" For the first time Tom has an intimation of company, of some intimate partner in perception. Momentarily he is checked. He looks again at the flowers. "Flowers? Why, of course, flowers." Together they look out of the same eyes. Again the evil genius whispers, "Flowers?" The seed of suspicion is to be the question. But Tom now raises the flowers nearer to his eyes almost violently as though his eyes were not his own. He is, however, not perturbed. The evil genius only shakes their head. "Did you ever hear of illusions?" says he.

Tom, still surprisingly good-natured, responds: "But you saw them, didn't you? Surely you can see through my eyes. Come, let us bury my nose deep in these blossoms, and take one long breath together. Then tell whether you can recognize these as flowers."

So they dunked the one nose. But the evil genius said "Huh!" as much as to say: What has all this seeming and smelling to do with it? Still he explained nothing. And Tom remained as confident of the flowers as he had been at the first. The little seeds of doubt, "Flowers? Flowers?" and again "Flowers?" and "Illusions?" and now this stick in the spokes, "Huh!" made Tom uneasy. He went on: "Oh, so you are one of these seers that has to touch everything. You're a tangibilite. Very well, here's my hand, let's finger these flowers. Careful! They're tender."

The evil genius was amused. He smiled inwardly and rippled in a shallow humor. To be taken for a materialist! As though the grand illusionist was not a spirit! Nevertheless, he realized that though deception is easy where the lies are big enough (where had he heard that before?), a few scattered, questioning words are not enough to make guile grow. He was tempted to make a statement, and he did. He said, "Your flowers are nothing but illusions."

"My flowers illusions?" exclaimed Tom, and he took up the bowl and placed it before a mirror. "See," said he, "here are the flowers and here, in the mirror, is an illusion. There's a difference surely. And you with my eyes, my nose, and my fingers can tell what that difference is. Pollen on your fingers touching the illusion? Send Milly the flowers in the mirror? Set a bee to suck honey out of this glass? You know all this as well as I do. I can tell flowers from illusions, and my flowers, as you now plainly see, are not illusions."

The evil genius was now sorely tried. He had his make-believe, but he also had his pride. Would he now risk the make-believe to save his pride? Would he explain? He explained.

"Tom," he said, "notice. The flowers in the mirror look like flowers, but they only look like flowers. We agree about that. The flowers before the mirror also look like flowers. But they, you say, are flowers because they also smell like flowers and they feel like flowers, as though they would be any more flowers because they also like flowers multiply. Imagine a mirror such that it reflected not only the looks of flowers, but also their fragrance and their petal surfaces, and then you smelled and touched, and the flowers before the mirror would be just like the flowers in the mirror. Then you could see immediately that the flowers before the mirror are illusions just as those in the mirror are illusions. As it is now, it is clear that the flowers in the mirror are thin illusions, and the flowers before the mirror are thick. Thick illusions are the best for deception. And they may be as thick as you like. From them you may gather pollen, send them to Milly, and foolish bees may sleep in them."

But Tom was not asleep. "I see that what you mean by thin illusions is what I mean by illusions, and what you mean by thick illusions is what I mean by flowers. So when you say that my flowers are your thick illusions this doesn't bother me. And as for your mirror that mirrors all layers of your thick illusions, I shouldn't call that a mirror at all. It's a duplicator, and much more useful than a mirror, provided you can control it. But I do suppose that when you speak of thick illusions you do mean that thick illusions are related to something you call flowers in much the same way that the thin illusions are related to the thick ones. Is that true?"

The evil genius was now diction-deep in explanations and went on. "In the first place let me assure you that these are not flowers. I destroyed all flowers. There are no flowers at all. There are only thin and thick illusions of flowers. I can see your flowers in the mirror, and I can smell and touch the flowers before the mirror. What I cannot smell and touch, having seen as in the mirror, is not even thick illusion. But if I cannot also *cerpicio* what I see, smell, touch, etc., what I have then seen is not anything real. *Esse est cerpici.* I just now tried to *cerpicio* your flowers, but there was nothing there. Man is after all a four- or five- or six-sense creature and you cannot expect much from so little."

Tom rubbed his eyes and his ears tingled with an eighteenth-century disturbance. Then he stared at the flowers. "I see," he said, "that this added sense of yours has done wickedly with our language. You do not mean by illusion what we mean, and neither do you mean by flowers what we mean. As for *cerpicio* I wouldn't be surprised if you'd made up that word just to puzzle us. In any case what you destroyed is what, according to you, you used to *cerpicio*. So there is nothing for you to *cerpicio* any more. But there still are what we mean by flowers. If your intention was to deceive, you must learn the language of those you are to deceive. I should say that you are like the doctor who prescribes for his patients what is so bad for himself and is then surprised at the health of his patients." And he pinned a flower near their nose.

The evil genius, discomfited, rode off on a corpuscle. He had failed. He took to an artery, made haste to the pineal exit, and was gone. Then "sun by sun" he fell. And he regretted his mischief.

I have tried in this essay to understand the boast of the evil genius. His boast was that he could deceive, deceive about "the heavens, the earth, the colors, figures, sound, and all other external things." In order to do this I have tried to bring clearly to mind what deception and such deceiving would be like. Such deception involves illusions and such deceiving involves the creation of illusions. Accordingly I have tried to imagine the evil genius engaged in the practice of deception, busy in the creation of illusions. In the first adventure everything is plain. The evil genius employs paper, paper making believe it's many other things. The effort to deceive, ingenuity in deception, being deceived by paper, detecting the illusion—all these are clearly understood.

It is the second adventure, however, which is more crucial. For in this instance it is assumed that the illusion is of such a kind that no seeing, no touching, no smelling, are relevant to detecting the illusion. Nevertheless the evil genius sees, touches, smells, and does detect the illusion. He made the illusion; so, of course, he must know it. How then does he know it? The evil genius has a sense denied to men. He senses the flower-in-itself, Milly-in-her-self, etc. So he creates illusions made up of what can be seen, heard, smelled, etc., illusions all because when seeing, hearing, and smelling have seen, heard, and smelled all, the special sense senses nothing. So what poor human beings sense is the illusion of what only the evil genius can sense. This is formidable. Nevertheless, once again everything is clear. If we admit the special sense, then we can readily see how it is that the evil genius should have been so confident. He has certainly created his own illusions, though he has not himself been deceived. But neither has anyone else been deceived. For human beings do not use the word "illusion" by relation to a sense with which only the evil genius is blessed.

I said that the evil genius had not been deceived, and it is true that he has not been deceived by his own illusions. Nevertheless he was deceived in boasting that he could deceive, for his confidence in this is based upon an ignorance of the difference between our uses of the words, "heavens," "earth," "flowers," "Milly," and "illusions" of these things, and his own uses of these words. For though there certainly is an analogy between our own uses and his, the difference is quite sufficient to explain his failure at grand deception. We can also understand how easily Tom might have been taken in. The dog over the water dropped his meaty bone for a picture on the water. Tom, however, dropped nothing at all. But the word "illusion" is a trap.

I began this essay uneasily, looking at my hands and saying "no hands," blinking my eyes and saying "no eyes." Everything I saw seemed to me like something Cheshire, a piece of cheese, for instance, appearing and disappearing in the leaves of the tree. Poor kitty! And now? Well. . . .

14

Raymond Smullyan, "Dream or Reality?" from *5000 B.C. and Other Philosophical Fantasies*

Raymond Smullyan (b. 1919) is a mathematical logician and philosopher. He has also had careers in music and magic. He has taught at Princeton, Dartmouth, the City University of New York, and Indiana University. He is the author of thirteen books, including This Book Needs No Title, Recursion Theory for Metamathematics, The Tao Is Silent, Theory of Formal Systems, The Lady or the Tiger and Other Logic Puzzles, *and* Gödel's Incompleteness Theorems. *His main work,* Diagonalization and Self-Reference, *was recently published by the Oxford University Press.*

To distinguish the real from the unreal, one must experience them both.

S. Gorn's *Compendium of Rarely Used Clichés*[1]

SKEPTIC: You claim that you see a chair. How do you know that you see a chair?

SUBJECT: I never said that I know that I see a chair; I merely said that I *see* a chair. I am not as sure that I know that I see a chair as I am that I see a chair. To me, seeing is more immediate than knowing.

SKEPTIC: Suppose I prove to you that you don't see a chair?

SUBJECT: No proof can convince me since I already know that I do see a chair.

SKEPTIC: Ah, I've caught you! You do claim you *know* you see a chair.

From Raymond Smullyan, *5000 B.C. and Other Philosophical Fantasies*, New York, St. Martin's Press, 1983.

1. S. Gorn. *Compendium of Rarely Used Clichés* (unpublished and used with permission of the author).

SUBJECT: I never denied knowing it; I merely said that I am less sure that I know it than that I am seeing the chair.

SKEPTIC: And you would still claim to see the chair even if I proved to you that you don't?

SUBJECT: Of course I would!

SKEPTIC: Then you are being irrational.

SUBJECT: Not really.

SKEPTIC: Can you prove that you are seeing a chair?

SUBJECT: Of course not! Or rather, I should ask, "Prove it from what premises?"

SKEPTIC: Can you at least prove that it is probable?

SUBJECT: Probable? I don't even know what it means to say that it is *probable* that I am seeing a chair. What I say is that I *am* seeing a chair.

SKEPTIC: But how do you know that you are seeing a chair?

SUBJECT: You asked me that before. Let me say this: First of all, I am not completely clear that I understand the meaning of *how I know* anymore than *how I see.* But to the extent that I do understand it, I can honestly say that I do not know *how* I know that I see a chair.

SKEPTIC: So you don't know *how* you know you see a chair, and you admit you can't prove you see a chair, yet you stubbornly maintain that you see a chair.

SUBJECT: Of course!

SKEPTIC: Then you are being dogmatic!

SUBJECT: Perhaps.

SKEPTIC: But do you really want to be dogmatic? Just think of what dogma leads to! Think of fascism, communism, and the Spanish Inquisition.

SUBJECT: Oh, come on now; these are examples of intolerance, not just dogmatism!

SKEPTIC: But what is the difference between dogmatism and intolerance?

SUBJECT: The present case is as good an illustration as any. One might label my dogged belief that I see a chair *dogmatic* (though I am not sure this would be correct), but surely no one in his right mind would label this belief of mine *an act of intolerance!*

SKEPTIC: The reason that I cannot accept your statement that you see a chair is that I doubt the existence of chairs. I think, however, that one can translate your statement into another form whose truth I would accept. I think that what you are *really* trying to say is that you are having a certain visual sensation—the so-called sensation of seeing a chair.

SUBJECT: If it makes you happy to translate it into those terms, by all means do so! *I* would not think of saying it this way. It *may* be also true—in fact, it probably is true—that I am having this so-called sensation. But again, as I see it, the notion of sensation is a far more sophisticated concept than just seeing and leads to a considerable number of philosophical problems and ambiguities. To a phenomenalist or idealist, a sensation is an immediate element of experience. To a materialistic realist, a sensation is a certain brain state or cerebral phenomenon, which seems to me to be something completely different. At any rate, the sort of statements that I most immediately understand are things like, "I see a chair," "I see a table," and so forth. I understand statements involving terms like *sensation* mainly to the extent to which I can translate them into such primitive statements.

SKEPTIC: But would it not be a more secure basis for philosophy to start out assuming only the things one really knows, like one's own sensations? No one but you can know whether you have a sensation or not. So if you say you have a given sensation, it cannot be reasonably denied. But you have absolutely no basis for claiming to know that the sensation is *of* something.

SUBJECT: This whole way of starting out philosophy is, to my mind, the worst one possible. To start out with one's *sensations* (or sense data) as the primary known realities! Children, who to my mind are the best philosophers, don't do anything like that. They talk about *objects,* not *sensations* of objects. Once you start out with sensations as the given, then you get involved in the whole nightmare of worrying about the very problem you raised: Are there objects corresponding to these sensations, or are there just free-floating sensations, so to speak? Then the problem arises as to what these objects are really like: How do they resemble our sensations of them, how do they cause the sensations of them, and for that matter what real evidence do we have for their very existence? Is our evidence probabilistic, or must we accept objects as an act of "animal faith"? Kant thought it a scandal of philosophy that the existence of external objects had never been satisfactorily proved. But to me, the search for a proof is utterly ridiculous. I directly perceive the objects; what more could I want? I don't *perceive* sensations at all. At least, the things I perceive I don't call *sensations* but *objects,* like this chair. I can assure you that if I did not perceive this chair directly, then absolutely *no* proof for its existence

would carry the slightest conviction with me. I honestly regard it as
pathological to require proofs of things one already knows.

An important consideration has just occurred to me. There is another
way—a totally different way—of understanding the statement, "I see
a chair," than the one I had in mind, that is, the way it would be
understood by a physicist qua physicist, which is a statement about the
physical world, made within the framework of physics. This *secondary*
interpretation, which to my utter amazement is regarded as primary
by some philosophers, states that my body is now facing the chair, I
am awake with open eyes, light rays are reflected from the chair that
form an image on my retina, causing physiological changes in my optic
nerve, brain, and so forth. If this "physicalistic" interpretation of my
statement is what you understood, then I can well understand your
labeling my sureness of it an unfounded dogma—indeed, I would
agree! I *believe* that this secondary interpretation also holds, but I cannot
possibly *know* it in the absolute sense that I know the other. Indeed,
I know this only secondhand, that is, on the testimony of scientists. I
have never seen my brain or optic nerve and only know of them
from authorities I trust. Incidentally, my objections to analyzing the
statement, "I see a chair," into objects and relationships does not apply
to the "physicalistic" interpretation; indeed, this interpretation does
put together things like human bodies, chairs, light rays, optic nerves,
brains, and so forth. Although I also clearly understand this secondary
interpretation, it is a far more involved business than the primary
interpretation, and I am able to understand this secondary interpretation only by analyzing it ultimately in terms of experience statements
in their primary sense.

SKEPTIC: Since you make this sharp dichotomy between what you
call the primary and secondary interpretations of experience statements
and claim such an important difference between them, how in discourse
do you make clear which meaning you have in mind?

SUBJECT: With philosophers—particularly so-called materialists—
this is usually the most difficult thing in the world! With most people—
especially with children—there is no difficulty whatsoever since they
usually understand experience sentences only in the primary sense. Of
course, primitive people—as well as all people who lived before the
rise of science and so knew nothing about optic nerves and brains—
can understand such statements *only* in the primary sense.

The situation seems to me well-nigh tragic. People in their childhood
understand only the primary interpretation of experience statements.

But at some stage of their development, particularly those who study science, they become aware of the secondary interpretation. They learn that one sees a chair when and only when one's physical brain is in a certain state. This is an exciting realization. But unfortunately certain people—those who become materialists—tend to identify the two meanings and cannot subsequently separate them. It may be possible that they even forget after awhile the primary meaning altogether, but I think this in fact unlikely. If they did, it almost would be too frightening to imagine. It would be as if someone like Alberich traded love for gold, and after living in the world of gold for awhile totally forgot what love was even like except in the purely operational sense of understanding how people behave when they are in love. But as I said, I doubt that my fears have any real basis. To use an analogy, a blind physicist knows what the word *red* means only in the *secondary sense;* a sighted child, knowing no physics, knows the word in the *primary* sense. I doubt very much if a sighted adult who became blind could ever in his lifetime actually forget what *red* meant in the primary sense.

SKEPTIC: Isn't it unfortunate that the same words and phrases have these two very different senses and that our language doesn't have separate phrases for the two meanings?

SUBJECT: Extremely unfortunate! This is precisely one of the things that leads to so much confusion in philosophy!

SKEPTIC: Is there no way that you can explain your distinction of primary and secondary meanings of experience statements to, say, a hard-boiled materialist?

SUBJECT: They are obviously aware that I think that there are two meanings. The secondary meaning they already understand (at least I think they do). As for the primary meaning, those who are polite say, "I have no idea what you could possibly mean"; those who are more crass say, "You don't mean *anything at all;* you are just using meaningless words, you are simply talking nonsense!"

SKEPTIC: Could you give me an example?

SUBJECT: Yes. One way I can explain that my primary meaning of, "I see a chair," is totally different from the secondary meaning is this: Under the secondary meaning, it would be a total contradiction in terms to say that I might see a chair after my bodily death. But under the primary meaning, there is no contradiction at all. Whether I will see chairs after my death is (to my mind) simply an unknown fact, but it is inconceivable to me that the notion is *contradictory.* I am thinking of Schlick, who maintained that in principle there is no reason why he should not witness his own funeral. Ayer, on the other hand, held this notion to be self-contradictory. Clearly, Schlick was thinking of witnessing in what I term the primary sense, Ayer in the secondary sense. Obviously, Ayer would not accept my argument at all; he would not agree that his difference with Schlick showed that there are *two* senses of the phrase *I see* or *I witness*. He would deny that what I call the primary sense has any meaning at all.

SKEPTIC: Tell me, would you commit yourself to saying that you *know* that you see a chair?

SUBJECT: Yes, I would.

SKEPTIC: You realize, of course, that this commits you to saying that you know that you are now not dreaming.

SUBJECT: Not at all!

SKEPTIC: What!

SUBJECT: I said, "Not at all." I regard it as perfectly possible that right now I *am* dreaming.

SKEPTIC: Good God! Surely if you are dreaming right now, then you don't still maintain that you *now* see a chair!

SUBJECT: I most certainly do! In a million years, I would not *dream* of making my assertion that I see a chair dependent on the fact that I'm not dreaming.

SKEPTIC: But if you are now dreaming, then the chair you claim to see *doesn't even exist!*

SUBJECT: It most certainly *does* exist; I *see* it! It is one of the objects I am now dreaming about (assuming that I am actually dreaming).

SKEPTIC: But surely you don't maintain that the objects you dreamed about, say, last night, really exist!

SUBJECT: They may not exist now, but they sure as hell existed last night; I *saw* them!

SKEPTIC: No, no; you are putting it the wrong way! It's not that last night you *really* saw *dream* objects; it's that last night you *dreamed* that you saw *real* objects, but in fact you were wrong!

SUBJECT: Not at all; last night I really saw objects.

SKEPTIC: Would you call these objects real or not?

SUBJECT: This brings us to the heart of the matter. Look, I don't use such words as *real, unreal, dream, nondream, real world, unreal world* in an absolute sense but only in a relative sense. Let me explain.

What do I mean when I say that right now I may be dreaming? This should be explained first. Well, last night I went to sleep and then saw all sorts of objects. This morning I woke up, and where are all these objects? They are nowhere to be found in the world I now experience. So I tend to declare them unreal and the state I was in last night a "dream state," or the world I experienced last night a dream world. When I say that I may be dreaming now, all I mean is that I am open to the possibility that at some future time I may be in a state in which I regard my present state as I did my state last night. In other words, the experience of having gone from one state into another, in which the former state seemed to be unreal, has happened to me many times, and I cannot see why it cannot happen to me again with regard to the very state I am in now. It could be that in the next day or hour I could again have the experience I call *waking up* and regard my present state as unreal. In fact, I don't expect this to happen the next hour, day, week, month, or several years. But when my body dies, I am less sure that I will not enter a state relative to which my present state is a dream. And this state in turn may prove to be unreal relative to some future state, and so forth ad infinitum.

At any rate, I no longer believe in any absolute notion of what is real. I only think of the reality of a state or of an object as relative to some other state. Thus, the very question of whether I am now dreaming in some absolute sense is (to me) meaningless. I can only consider such a purely empirical question as whether or not my present state will one day seem unreal. Every state is real relative to itself. To me, it is an open question whether or not every state may be unreal relative to some other state.[2]

SKEPTIC: I must say, your idea terrifies me! Look, before we started talking about dreams, I thought that the whole time you were defending the philosophy of common sense in an uninhibitedly dogmatic manner. You *see* chairs; therefore, there *are* chairs, and so forth. Then you pull this complete reversal and come up with this ultrafantastic *idealism!* I must say, I am completely bewildered, and it will take me awhile to get over the shock.

2. To the mathematical reader, the situation as described has a resemblance to conclusions some mathematical logicians have drawn from the Skolem-Löwenheim theorem. This theorem is to the effect that no axiom system (of first order logic) can compel the domain of interpretation to be nondenumerable. This led Skolem and others to believe that the very notion of nondenumerability has no absolute meaning.

SUBJECT: I don't regard this idea as either fantastic or idealistic.

SKEPTIC: Of course it is idealistic to say that *nothing* has absolute reality, that reality is only *relative* to something else!

SUBJECT: This is not idealism.

SKEPTIC: Look, I'm not going to quibble with you over terminology. Maybe it shouldn't be called *idealism* but simply *crazy and fantastic.* All right, I admit that on purely logical grounds, your position is no more disprovable than, say, something like solipsism. At least, at the moment I am not clever enough to find an actual inconsistency in your doctrine. So on rational grounds, I cannot refute you. But on psychological grounds I find the doctrine extremely dangerous. Frankly, the idea that one day I might wake up or be in another state relative to which all the objects and people around me that I have come to know and love should turn out to be *unreal* fills me with utter horror and totally shatters my feelings of security.

SUBJECT: I am glad that you brought up psychological factors because I think that they are most relevant. My psychological reaction is the very opposite of yours; to me, the belief in some absolute reality would make *me* highly insecure!

SKEPTIC: Why on earth should it do that?

SUBJECT: Because once I believed in this thing called *reality*, then I would start worrying about whether the things that appeared real to me really were real!

SKEPTIC: Why can't you just *know* that they are real as I do?

SUBJECT: Hey, I thought *you* were the skeptic! It seems in some ways that I am more skeptical than you.

SKEPTIC: You sure are! Indeed, your whole method of philosophizing is the strangest mixture of dogmatism and skepticism I have ever seen! About certain things you are totally dogmatic and about all other things—all things that are not *your* dogmas—you are skeptical.

SUBJECT: But of course! How could I be anything other than dogmatic about things that I know and skeptical about things that I don't?

SKEPTIC: But tell me honestly, why are you skeptical that the things before you are real in any absolute sense?

SUBJECT: When you use the word *why*, I am not sure whether you are asking for a psychological explanation as to how I got this way, or whether you are asking for my epistemological reasons. Let me first consider the former, which brings us back to the very important point you raised about feeling secure. Don't you see that once I admitted an absolute reality, I would have all the nightmarish problems about whether I am *really* awake or not. But without this category, all these awful problems don't even arise!

SKEPTIC: But ignoring a problem does not solve it! I can't reject the notion of reality just to avoid facing problems. Besides, the very thought that there is no such thing as reality itself makes me insecure.

SUBJECT: Originally, you told me that my philosophy, though possibly consistent, was dangerous because it leads to psychological insecurity. In other words, your immediate reason for rejecting it was that it makes *you* feel insecure. But now when I tell you that it makes *me* feel secure, you say these are not legitimate grounds for accepting it. Are you being quite fair?

SKEPTIC: No, you are right.

SUBJECT: I would like to say more about feeling secure. It is difficult for me to believe that what really makes you (or me, for that matter) feel insecure is that the objects we both see lack this property of absolute reality. Isn't the real fear that at some future time we may come to believe or to *feel* the unreality of the objects we both now perceive?

SKEPTIC: That is certainly part of it, but not all.

SUBJECT: Well, let me put it this way. Suppose God himself (or any being you would take to be both omniscient and truthful) would now come down to earth and say to you, "There is indeed such a thing as absolute reality. But, for certain reasons, I am not going to tell you whether any of the things or people you now perceive are real. This much I promise you, however: Never will you have the experience of one day being in a state relative to which your present state will appear like a dream. In other words, if you are dreaming now, then—unlike the dreams you have had before—you will never know it, not even in the afterlife, if there is one." My question now is whether this answer would satisfy you.

SKEPTIC: I'm afraid not. This would mean that I never would know which things were real and which were not.

SUBJECT: Well, suppose God then said, "All right, I'll tell you after all. Everything you now see *is* real." Would that satisfy you?

SKEPTIC: It would still not satisfy me, because I might be afraid that I was only dreaming that God spoke to me.

SUBJECT: Hey, it seems that *you* are the one who is *really* insecure! Insecure, that is, in *your* philosophy, not mine!

SKEPTIC: I'm afraid you are right. Well, I guess what I need is to have *faith* that I am now not dreaming.

SUBJECT: Ah! That is precisely the difference between your approach and mine. I don't want my feeling of security to have to depend on any act of faith. I have always thought of faith as somehow "whistling in the dark."

SKEPTIC: But how without some act of faith can you know you are not now dreaming?

SUBJECT: I told you before that I use the word *dream* only in a relative sense. But a point that I think may be important has just occurred to me. When I suggest the possibility that reality is only relative, that every world (or state) may be unreal relative to some other world, does this idea make you feel that the present world (the one we are now in and see) is less real than you would normally feel, or that other worlds are more real? In other words, do you feel that I am trying to make the present world more fantasylike, dreamlike, or chimerical or that I am trying to make fantasy worlds appear more real?

SKEPTIC: Why, the former, of course. If I believed that every world was unreal relative to some other world, then I would feel that *all* worlds, including this one, were unreal.

SUBJECT: Oh, if that is your reaction, then I certainly don't blame you for totally rejecting the idea. I was thinking of it the opposite way! I was not trying to "derealify" this world but rather to "realify" so-called nonreal worlds. Why can't you see it in this light?

SKEPTIC: I don't know; the idea is quite new to me. I would have to think about it.

SUBJECT: You see, there is one important difference in our attitudes. Suppose for the moment that there really is an afterlife and that in the first state we enter the present world is unreal relative to that state. Your reaction will be very different from mine. You will say, "How surprising; I thought my previous state was real, but I was wrong; I was *deceived.*" I will say, "Just as I thought, the last state was real and interesting while it lasted, but was *impermanent.* Too bad, I guess nothing lasts forever."

I really think that the notion of permanence is the key to the whole business. Let me ask you another question. Suppose you were on another planet—call it Planet *A*—on which all the inhabitants, including yourself, slept half the time (instead of roughly a third of the time, as we do here). Now suppose at the end of each day on Planet *A* you undressed, went to bed, fell asleep, and found yourself in a totally different body—call it Body *B*—on a totally different planet called

Planet *B*. You would spend a day on Planet *B*, at the end of which your *B*-body would undress, get into bed, go to sleep, and then you would return to State *A*. Let us assume that your existence in State *B* were just as consistent and coherent as in State *A*. When in State *A* you put some object on the desk and went to sleep, the next morning it was still there, and the same held for State *B*. Assume also that this state of affairs has been going on all your life; indeed, you were unable to recall whether your life started in State *A* or State *B*. I repeat, each state had the same coherent internal structure. Let us say that science and psychology were about equally advanced in both worlds. The scientists of World *A* would assure you that your thought processes were nothing more nor less than certain physiological events in your brain—call it Brain *A*. They would tell you that when you went to sleep and "dreamed" you were on Planet *B*, this "dream" was nothing more than certain physical events taking place in Brain *A*. But the scientists of Planet *B* would tell you exactly the same thing in reverse; all your thoughts were nothing but events in Brain *B*. Moreover, they would tell you that Brain *A* doesn't really exist at all; those on Planet *A* would tell you that Brain *B* doesn't really exist except as a figment of the imagination of Brain *A*. I can even imagine the psychiatrists of both planets each diagnosing you as schizophrenic for believing in the reality of the other state; perhaps each would offer you some medication that would permanently cure you of your "illusion" concerning the other state.

Now, you must admit that under these circumstances your whole notion of reality would probably be very different. What would you believe? That either State *A* or State *B* was real and the other illusory, but you couldn't decide which? Or maybe that both states were real— that there could be, so to speak, two disjoint realities? Or perhaps you would suspect that both states were unreal and that your *real* state— State *C*—was something very different yet? Or maybe that *no* states are real? Don't you think that you would reject the very notion of reality as meaningless and would simply settle for the realization that each of the two states was internally real but that neither one was real relative to the other and that the only common bond would be that you experience them both?

SKEPTIC: Of course, *had* I lived such a life, my views on reality would probably have been very different. But the fact is that I have *not* lived such a weird life. So why should I let my views be influenced by the hypothetical situation you have just been spinning out, which itself is just a sheer fantasy? I'd like to know what you are really driving at. Tell me honestly, why are you so intent on trying to relativize the notion of reality? You said before something about having some epistemological reasons for rejecting any absolute notion of reality. What now are these reasons?

SUBJECT: My reason for rejecting it is very simply that I have absolutely no reasons for accepting it. Indeed, I don't even know what the notion really means! I have no idea how I can use the notion. Suppose I enter a new place and see a wooden chair. At least it *looks* wooden to me, but then it occurs to me that it may not be really wooden; perhaps it is cleverly painted papier mâché. In this sense, the word *really* means something quite definite to me; I know how to go about testing it. So I go over to the chair, inspect it more closely, feel it, and so forth, and conclude, "Yes, it really is made of wood." But now, what in the world would it mean for me to ask, "But is this chair real, or is it only illusory?" What test can I possibly perform to find out if the chair has this mysterious property of being real?

SKEPTIC: Why is it that you, who are usually so hostile to positivism, take such a positivist attitude toward this question?

SUBJECT: Because in this regard, I feel that the positivists have something of value to contribute. Incidentally, concerning my "hostile" attitude toward positivism, I think that I should state clearly that I divide positivists into two types, which I call *dogmatic positivists* and *skeptical positivists*. The dogmatic positivist will say about any word, phrase, or sentence whose meaning he cannot understand that it is meaningless or nonsensical. The skeptical positivist will instead be skeptical that it has any meaning or will wonder what the meaning could be. I am perfectly sympathetic to the skeptical positivist; it is only the dogmatic positivist of whom I am totally intolerant. After all, since I am dogmatic myself, it is only natural that I cannot tolerate any dogmas that conflict with mine.

But coming back to the notion of absolute reality, I, like the skeptical positivist, do not really understand what the notion is and indeed have some doubts that the notion has any real meaning. But I am not prepared to say that it is meaningless. The notion of absolute reality somehow reminds me of the notion of absolute position in space or absolute motion in space. When people first hear from the physical relativist that there is no such thing as bodies moving through something called *space*, but that bodies move only relative to each other, the reaction is often something of a shock; the new idea somehow seems counterintuitive. The dogmatic type of relativist will say, "There is no such thing as absolute motion; this is just an antiquated notion." The more modest and reasonable type of relativist, when asked, "How do you know that there is no such thing as absolute motion through space?" will reply, "I cannot say for sure that there is no such thing but merely that I do not know what it is and can see no possible way to use it in science. The subject matter of physical science is simply the description of how objects move relative to each other. And nowhere can I see how the hypothesis of absolute motion can be used in this study."

I have similar feelings about a chair's being real. Saying that it is relatively real is quite different. Again, this notion is related to the notion of permanence. I will put it this way: I certainly do have a notion of something appearing real or seeming real to me. For example, the chair I see before me certainly seems real to me. The chair I saw yesterday while I was awake seemed real to me then and still seems real to me in retrospect. But the objects I saw last night in my sleep seemed real to me then (at least as far as I now remember) but do not seem real to me now. So it is perfectly meaningful to ask whether I may *in the future* be in a state in which the chair I presently perceive will then seem unreal to me.

SKEPTIC: But this again is something you cannot now test.

SUBJECT: Of course I can't possibly test the chair to find out whether *in the future* it will seem real to me any more than I can now test it to determine whether in the future some rock will be hurled through the window and demolish it.[3] But both notions seem to me perfectly meaningful.

SKEPTIC: Perhaps your idea of relative reality is not so bad after all. It also may not be a bad idea to define something to be absolutely real to a given observer if it is in your sense permanently real, that is, if at no future time will it seem unreal.

Still, I am vaguely disquieted. I must say that I have a lingering intuition that there is something more to reality than a mere reduction

---

3. This reminds me of the beautiful Haiku poem:

There is nothing in the voice of the cicada
To indicate how long it will live.

to a permanent set of appearances. Do you honestly maintain that you have *no* such intuition?

SUBJECT: To be absolutely honest, I do have such a lingering intuition. But for that matter, I must also confess that I still have left *some* remnants of my childhood intuition concerning absolute motion.

SKEPTIC: So how do you reconcile these intuitions with your relativist position?

SUBJECT: I, as it were, hold such intuitions in abeyance. Incidentally, my intuition concerning absolute motion is much weaker than my intuition concerning absolute reality. Indeed, by now it has practically disappeared. But with the notion of absolute reality I am less sure that there is nothing to it. What should one do with such intuitions, intuitions that conflict with reason or with stronger intuitions? I do not believe in being overly brutal and harsh—even with oneself—and tearing out those intuitions that one regretfully realizes are not in complete harmony with one's general world view. I have far too much respect for *any* intuition to wish to "murder" it. So I let such intuitions, so to speak, lie asleep. I say to myself, "It is difficult to know what absolute reality can be, other than what I have suggested. But then again it appears possibly to have some other meaning. But I don't know how to work with such a meaning. So I will suspend final judgment until I have more knowledge."

SKEPTIC: I think your attitude is very reasonable. Still, I would love to know just a little more about your intuition of absolute reality. Strange, isn't it, that *I* have been defending this notion, and you have been attacking it. Yet you have so convinced me that this notion is unsatisfactory that I have to appeal to *you* for help in finding out what *I* mean by *absolutely real!* What is it you are looking for, and how will you recognize it if you ever find out? Or do you feel that in principle you never can?

SUBJECT: No, I would not say that in principle I never can find it, though I have as yet no idea of how I can or even just what it is that I seek. I am not one to go along with the idea that it is hopeless to find something unless one knows precisely what it is that one is looking for. So it is with the notion of absolute reality. I told you about my skeptical reasons for doubting that there is really anything to the notion, and so I am unable to use it in my actual life. Yet, as I have confessed, I still sometimes have the haunting feeling that I am overlooking something crucial, that I may be missing something of extreme importance. How can I find it? God only knows! There is nothing more at present that I can possibly do. But who knows. Maybe one day the idea, if there really is any idea, might dawn on me. Perhaps through further advance of science, through a more refined logical analysis of the question, or through something like a sudden mystical insight, it might happily happen that I will say, "Ah of course! How simple! So that's what reality *really* is!"

15

Octavio Paz,
"Certainty,"
from *Configurations*,
trans. Sharon Sieber

Octavio Paz (b. 1914) is the major Mexican poet, writer, and philosopher of his generation. He gave the Charles Eliot Norton Lectures at Harvard, which were published as Children of the Mire *in 1974. He won the Nobel Prize for Literature in 1990.*

Sharon Sieber teaches Spanish at Idaho State University. She is currently working on a critical study of Paz.

Certeza

Si es real la luz blanca
De esta lámpara, real
La mano que escribe, son reales
Los ojos que miran lo escrito?

De una palabra a la otra
Lo que digo se desvanece.
Yo sé que estoy vivo
Entre dos paréntesis.

From *Configurations*, New York, New Directions, 1971, by kind permission of Octavio Paz and New Directions.

Certainty

If it is real the white light
Of this lamp, real
The hand which writes, are they real
The eyes which look upon the written?

From one word to the next
What I say vanishes.
I know that I am alive
Between two parentheses.

Further Readings

Ayer, A. J., *The Problem of Knowledge,* London, Penguin, 1956, esp. Ch. 2, "Scepticism and Certainty."

———, "Wittgenstein on Certainty," in Godfrey Vesey (ed.), *Understanding Wittgenstein.* Royal Institute of Philosophy Lectures, Vol. 7, 1972–1973, London, Macmillan, 1974.

Cornford, F. M., *Plato's Theory of Knowledge,* London, Routledge & Kegan Paul, 1935.

Dewey, John, *The Quest for Certainty,* New York, Putnam, 1960.

Firth, Roderick, "The Anatomy of Certainty," *The Philosophical Review,* 76 (1967).

Frankfurt, H. G., "Philosophical Certainty," *The Philosophical Review,* 71 (1962).

Klein, Peter D., *Certainty: A Refutation of Cartesian Scepticism,* Minneapolis, University of Minnesota Press, 1981.

———, "Certainty," in Jonathan Dancy and Ernest Sosa, *A Companion to Epistemology,* Oxford, Blackwell, 1992.

Locke, John, *An Essay Concerning Human Understanding,* ed. Peter H. Nidditch, Oxford, Oxford University Press, 1975, Book IV, Ch. 1–4.

Malcolm, Norman, *Knowledge and Certainty,* Englewood Cliffs, Prentice Hall, N. J., 1963.

Miller, R., "Absolute Certainty," *Mind,* 97 (1978).

Moore, G. E., "A Defence of Common Sense" and "Proof of an External World," in *Philosophical Papers,* London, Allen and Unwin, 1959.

———, "Being Certain that One Is in Pain," *Selected Writings,* ed. Thomas Baldwin, London, Routledge, 1993.

Morawetz, Thomas, *Wittgenstein and Knowledge,* Amherst, University of Massachusetts Press, 1978.

Rollins, C. D., "Certainty," in *The Encyclopedia of Philosophy,* ed. Paul Edwards, Vol. I, New York, Macmillan, 1967.

Stroll, Avrum, *Moore and Wittgenstein on Certainty,* Oxford, Oxford University Press, 1994.

Wittgenstein, Ludwig, *Last Writings on the Philosophy of Psychology,* Vol. 2, Oxford, Blackwell, 1992, esp. MS 174.